# Measuring up:
# The Performance of Canada's Youth in Reading, Mathematics and Science

## OECD PISA Study—First Results for Canadians aged 15

**Patrick Bussière,** *Human Resources Development Canada*
**Fernando Cartwright,** *Statistics Canada*
**Robert Crocker,** *Memorial University of Newfoundland*
**Xin Ma,** *University of Alberta*
**Jillian Oderkirk,** *Statistics Canada*
**Yanhong Zhang,** *Human Resources Development Canada*

D1378800

Published by authority of the Minister responsible for Statistics Canada

© Minister of Industry, 2001

December 2001

Catalogue no. 81-590-XPE

ISBN 0-660-18668-3

Catalogue no. 81-590-XIE

ISBN 0-662-31284-8

TORONTO PUBLIC LIBRARY
Sale of this book
supports literacy programs

Frequency: Irregular

Ottawa

Human Resources Development Canada, Council of Ministers of Education, Canada and Statistics Canada

*The data interpretations presented in this report are those of the authors and do not necessarily reflect those of the granting agencies or reviewers.*

National Library of Canada Canadian Cataloguing in Publication Data

Measuring up : the performance of Canada's youth in reading,
mathematics and science : OECD PISA study : first result for
Canadians aged 15

Issued also in French under title: À la hauteur : la performance des jeunes du
Canada en lecture, en mathématiques et en sciences : études PISA de
l'OCDE : premiers résultats pour les canadiens de 15 ans.
ISBN 0-660-18668-3 (paper)
ISBN 0-662-31284-8 (Internet)
CS81-590-XPE
CS81-590-XIE

1. High school students – Rating of – Canada.
2. Academic achievement – Canada  – Statistics.
3. Educational evaluation – Canada – Statistics.
I. Bussière, Patrick. II. Statistics Canada. II. Canada. Human Resources
Development Canada. III. Council of Ministers of Education (Canada).


LB3054.C3 M42 2001            373.26'2'0971
C2001-988012-X

# Acknowledgements

We would like to thank the students, parents, teachers and principals who gave of their time to participate in the 2000 OECD PISA study and the Youth in Transition Survey. The support for this Federal-Provincial collaborative project provided by members of the PISA-YITS Steering Committee and by the coordinators in each participating Ministry or Department of Education during all steps of the study is gratefully acknowledged. The dedication of the survey development, implementation, processing and methodology teams was essential to the project's success and is appreciated.

This publication was prepared jointly by Statistics Canada, Human Resources Development Canada and the Council of Ministers of Education, Canada and was supported financially by Human Resources Development Canada. The report has benefited from the input and comments of reviewers in provincial Ministries and Departments of Education, Human Resources Development Canada and Statistics Canada. The contribution of members of the joint Working Group on PISA-YITS Dissemination, Satya Brink, Patrick Bussière, Patrice de Broucker, Jeanine Bustros, Louis-Philippe Gaudreault, Dean Goodman, Douglas Hodgkinson, Marc Lachance, Michael Lerner, Scott Murray, Jillian Oderkirk, Monica Paabo and Dianne Pennock, is appreciated. The authors, Patrick Bussière, Fernando Cartwright, Robert Crocker, Xin Ma, Jillian Oderkirk and Yanhong Zhang, are thanked for their valued contribution to the dissemination of these first Canadian results. The staff of the Centre for Education Statistics at Statistics Canada, whose tireless efforts ensured a high standard of quality, are appreciated, particularly Mary Allen, Greg Anderson, Rosemarie Andrews, Marc Lachance and Sylvie Ouellette. A very special thank you is extended to Danielle Baum for her indispensable help in preparing the manuscript for publication. The contribution of editorial, communications, translation and dissemination services staff of Statistics Canada, Human Resources Development Canada and the Council of Ministers of Education, Canada was essential to the project's success and is appreciated.

# Note of Appreciation

Canada owes the success of its statistical system to the long-standing co-operation of Statistics Canada, the citizens of Canada, its businesses, governments and other institutions. Accurate and timely statistical information could not be produced without their continued co-operation and goodwill.

# Table of Contents

# Table of Contents

# Table of Contents

# Introduction

The skills and knowledge that Canadians bring to their jobs, and to our society, play an important role in determining our economic success and our overall quality of life. Evidence is mounting that the importance of skills and knowledge will continue to grow in the future. The shift from manufacturing to knowledge- and information-intensive service industries, advances in communication and production technologies, the wide diffusion of information technologies, falling trade barriers, and the globalization of financial markets and markets for products and services, have precipitated changes in the skills our economy requires. These include a rising demand for a strong set of foundation skills upon which further learning rests.

Elementary and secondary education systems play a central role in laying a solid base upon which subsequent knowledge and skills can be developed. Those students leaving secondary education without a strong foundation may experience difficulty accessing the postsecondary education system and the labour market and may be less prepared to succeed when learning opportunities are presented later in life. Those individuals with limited skills and without the tools needed to be effective learners throughout life risk economic marginalization.

Having invested huge sums in providing high quality universal elementary and secondary schooling, governments in industrialised countries, concerned about the relative effectiveness of these education systems, wanted to address these issues. Therefore, member governments of the Organisation for Economic Co-operation and Development (OECD) developed a common tool to improve their understanding of what makes young people—and education systems as a whole—successful. This tool is the Programme for International Student Assessment (PISA).

Information gathered through PISA enables a thorough comparative analysis of the skill level of students near the end of their compulsory education. PISA also permits exploration of the ways that skills vary across different social and economic groups and the factors that influence the level and distribution of skills within and between countries.

## The Canadian context

Canada's participation in the PISA study stems from many of the same concerns as have been expressed by other participating countries.

Canada invests significant public resources in the provision of elementary and secondary education. Among OECD countries, Canada ranks sixth in expenditure on elementary and secondary education as a proportion of GDP.[1] Canadians are concerned about the quality of education provided by elementary and secondary schools. How can expenditures be directed to achieve high levels of foundation skills and to potentially reduce social inequality?

Canada's economy is also evolving rapidly. For the past two decades the growth rate of knowledge-intensive occupations has been twice that of other occupations.[2] Even employees in traditional occupations have been asked to upgrade their skills to meet the rising skill demands of new organisational structures and production technologies. Primary and secondary education systems play a key role in generating the new supply of skills to meet this demand. The skills acquired by the end of compulsory schooling provide the essential foundation upon which we will develop the human capital needed to meet the economic and social challenges of the future.

Questions about educational effectiveness can be partly answered with data on the average performance of Canada's youth. However, two other questions can only be answered by examining the social distribution of skills: Who are the students whose performance places them at the lowest levels? Do particular groups or regions appear to be at greater risk? These are important questions because, among other things, skill acquisition during compulsory schooling influences access to postsecondary education and eventual success in the labour market.

Furthermore, understanding how the knowledge and skills acquired by the end of compulsory education affect future life transitions, including participation in higher education and the labour market, can only be achieved by examining the life paths of students as they progress from youth to adulthood. To answer these questions, Human Resources Development Canada, the Council of Ministers of Education Canada and Statistics Canada decided to integrate the PISA skill assessment with the Canadian Youth in Transition Survey (YITS).

## What is PISA?

The OECD initiated the Programme for International Student Assessment (PISA) to provide policy-oriented international indicators of the skills and knowledge of 15-year-old students. [3] PISA is a collaborative effort among OECD member countries to regularly assess youth outcomes in three domains—reading literacy, mathematical literacy and scientific literacy—through common international tests. International experts from OECD member countries have agreed on the following definitions for each domain:

**Reading literacy:** Understanding, using and reflecting on written texts, in order to achieve one's goals, to develop one's knowledge and potential, and to participate in society.

**Mathematical literacy:** The capacity to identify, to understand, and to engage in mathematics and make well-founded judgements about the role that mathematics plays, as needed for individuals' current and future private life, occupational life, social life with peers and relatives and as a constructive, concerned and reflective citizen.

**Scientific literacy:** The capacity to use scientific knowledge, to identify questions and to draw evidence-based conclusions in order to understand and help make decisions about the natural world and the changes made to it through human activity.

PISA assessed the degree to which students approaching the end of their compulsory education have acquired some of the knowledge and skills that are essential for full participation in society. PISA hopes to answer the following questions:

- How well are young adults prepared to meet the challenges of the future?
- Are they able to analyse, reason and communicate their ideas effectively?
- Do they have the capacity to continue learning throughout life?
- Are some kinds of teaching and school organization more effective than others?

Three PISA cycles have been planned, each one focussing on a different literacy domain. In 2000 the major focus was reading literacy, with mathematical and scientific literacy as minor domains. Mathematical and scientific literacy will be focused on in 2003 and 2006, respectively.

## PISA 2000

Thirty-two countries[4] participated in PISA 2000. The survey instruments were translated and adapted from two source languages, English and French, into 17 different languages. In most countries, between 4,500 and 10,000 15-year-olds participated in PISA.

In Canada, approximately 30,000 15-year-old students from more than 1,000 schools participated. The large Canadian sample was needed to produce reliable estimates for each province[5], and for both English and French language school systems in Manitoba, Ontario, Quebec, New Brunswick and Nova Scotia. The assessment was administered in schools, during regular school hours, in April and May 2000.

The PISA 2000 survey included a direct assessment of students' skills through reading, mathematics and science tests. A total of about seven hours of test items were administered, with each student taking a two-hour-long assessment consisting of different combinations of test items. The assessment focused mainly on reading, with the reading test giving three sub-test scores labelled *retrieving information, interpreting* and *reflecting*. Mathematics and science each had only a single score. In addition, as minor domains, there were fewer mathematics and science items included and these items were administered to a sub-sample of PISA participants.

Students also completed a 20-minute questionnaire focussing on factors contributing to student achievement and a three-minute questionnaire focussing on information technology. In addition, PISA 2000 included a questionnaire, which was administered to school principals, to collect information about the characteristics of participating schools.

A 30-minute self-completed contextual questionnaire from the Youth in Transition Survey was administered simultaneously to students in order to collect more information on their school experiences, their work activities and their relationships with others. A 30-minute interview was also conducted with parents.

> **More information on the PISA and YITS can be found on the website www.pisa.gc.ca. Included are documentation on the PISA framework from the OECD, the PISA and YITS project in Canada, PISA and YITS questionnaires, example PISA test items and other helpful references. A detailed technical appendix is also provided in the international OECD report, *Knowledge and Skills for Life: First results from the OECD Programme for International Student Assessment*.[6] Consult the OECD website www.pisa.oecd.org.**

## What is YITS?

The Youth in Transition Survey (YITS)[7] is a new Canadian longitudinal survey designed to examine the patterns of, and influences on, major transitions in young people's lives, particularly with respect to education, training and work. Survey results will help provide a deeper understanding of the nature and causes of challenges young people face as they manage their transitions. Information obtained from the survey will help to support policy planning and decision making that addresses problems.

YITS will examine key transitions in the lives of youth, such as the transition from high school to postsecondary education, from schooling to the labour market, and from the labour market to schooling. The factors that affect leaving school without graduating will be a focus, as will the effects of school experiences on educational and occupational outcomes, and the contribution of work experience programs, part-time jobs and volunteer activities. To collect this information, current plans for YITS are to survey youth every two years, over a period of several years. Accordingly, the second survey cycle of YITS is scheduled to take place in 2002.

Two different age groups are participating in YITS, a 15-year-old cohort and an 18- to 20-year-old cohort. The youth aged 15 who participated in YITS also participated in PISA 2000. The youth aged 18 to 20, who were surveyed in 2000 as part of the YITS project, did not participate in PISA. Results for the 18- to 20-year-old YITS cohort will be released in a separate report in early 2002.

## Why are YITS and PISA integrated in Canada?

As with most surveys, PISA 2000 provides a 'snapshot'—a picture at a specific point in time—of the group being surveyed. A longitudinal survey like YITS, on the other hand, involves surveying the same group of people over a period of time.

Collecting information on the same respondents over time makes it possible for YITS to study relationships between factors measured in one period (e.g., aspirations, attitudes, behaviours and achievement) with outcomes measured in future time periods (e.g., educational attainment, occupational outcomes and earnings). Moreover, the integration of YITS and PISA will enable the examination of the relationship between tested skills and knowledge and education and labour market outcomes of youth.

## Objectives and organization of the report

This report provides results of the PISA assessment of student performance in reading, science and mathematics at the provincial level that complement the information on national performance presented in the OECD international report, *Knowledge and Skills for Life – First results from the OECD Programme for International Student Assessment*. Wherever possible, an attempt has been made to put Canadian and provincial results into context by comparing and contrasting them with those of other countries.

Emphasis is placed on the average level of performance and on the distribution of achievement scores among specific social groups. This information is presented in Chapter 1 of this report. Chapter 2 focuses on how achievement is influenced by a student's personal characteristics and Chapter 3 explores the relationship between family characteristics and achievement. Chapter 4 presents an analysis of the relationship between school characteristics and achievement. Finally, the major findings and opportunities for further study are discussed in the conclusion.

This report is the first of a series of national reports conceived to capitalise on the wealth of information offered by the PISA study and the YITS.

| BOX 1 |
|---|

## Overview of PISA 2000

|  | INTERNATIONAL | CANADA |
|---|---|---|
| **Participating countries/provinces** | • 32 countries | • 10 provinces |
| **Population** | • Youth aged 15 | • Same |
| **Number of participating students** | • In general, 4,500 to 10,000 per country, with some exceptions for a total of over 250,000 students | • 30,000 students[8] |
| **Domains** | • Major: reading<br>• Minor: mathematics and science | • Same |
| **Languages in which the test was administered** | • 17 languages | • English and French |
| **International assessment** | • Two hours of direct skills assessment through reading, mathematics and science tests<br>• 20-minute self-completed contextual questionnaire administered to youth<br>• A school questionnaire administered to school principals | • Same |
| **International options** | • 3-minute optional self-completed questionnaire on information technology administered to students<br>• An optional self-completed questionnaire on self-regulated learning administered to students | • 3-minute optional self-completed questionnaire on information technology administered to students |
| **National options** | • Grade-based assessment<br><br>• Other options were undertaken in a limited number of countries | • A 30-minute YITS self-completed questionnaire administered to youth<br>• A 30-minute phone interview with a parent of the youth<br>• Items added to the school questionnaire |

# Notes

1. OECD (2000), *Education at a Glance*, Paris.

2. Lavoie, Marie, and Richard Roy (1998*), Employment in the Knowledge-Based Economy: A Growth Accounting Exercise for Canada*, Applied Research Branch Research Papers Series, Human Resources Development Canada catalogue no. R-98-8E, Ottawa.

3. The framework of PISA is presented in OECD (1999), *Measuring Student Knowledge and Skills: A New Framework for Assessment*, Paris.

4. Australia, Austria, Belgium, Brazil, Canada, Czech Republic, Denmark, Finland, France, Germany, Greece, Hungary, Iceland, Ireland, Italy, Japan, Korea, Latvia, Liechtenstein, Luxembourg, Mexico, The Netherlands, New Zealand, Norway, Poland, Portugal, Russian Federation, Spain, Sweden, Switzerland, United Kingdom, United States.

5. No data were collected in the three territories and on Indian Reserves.

6. OECD (2001), Knowledge and Skills for Life: First Results from the OECD Programme for International Student Assessment, Paris.

7. More information on the Youth in Transition Survey is provided in Human Resources Development Canada and Statistics Canada (2000*), Youth in Transition Survey: Project Overview*, Applied Research Branch Technical Paper, Human Resources Development Canada catalogue no. T-00-5E and Statistics Canada catalogue no. 81-588-X1E, Ottawa.

8. The number of participating students in each province was as follows: Newfoundland (2,281), Prince Edward Island (1,632), Nova Scotia (2,930), New Brunswick (2,963), Quebec (4,497), Ontario (4,290), Manitoba (2,599), Saskatchewan (2,716), Alberta (2,742), and British Columbia (3,037).

# Chapter 1

# The Achievement of Canadian Students within an International Context

This chapter presents results of the PISA assessment in reading, mathematics and science. It begins by comparing the achievement of 15-year-old students in Canada and the provinces with that of students in all participating countries. These initial comparisons focus on differences in average scores. Further analyses reveal the proportions of students at various levels of the scoring scale. The chapter also compares the performance of girls and boys. Finally, the performance of students enrolled in anglophone and francophone school systems, in the five provinces that sampled the two groups separately, is discussed.

## The performance of Canadian students in a global context

Overall, Canadian students performed well compared with students in most other countries, ranking second in reading, sixth in mathematics and fifth in science among 31 countries[1] (Figures 1.1 to 1.3). Canada is part of a cluster of countries that scored near the top in all areas. Only Finland performed significantly better than Canada in reading, only Korea and Japan performed significantly better than Canada in mathematics and only Korea, Japan and Finland performed significantly better in science. Differences between Canada and the top countries on the overall scale range from about 12 to 24 points.[2]

Table 1.0 shows the countries that performed significantly better than or about the same as Canada on the three tests. The average performance of students in all other countries was significantly below that of Canada.

| TABLE 1.0 | | |
|---|---|---|
| **Countries performing better than or about the same as Canada** | | |
| | Countries performing significantly better than Canada | Countries performing about the same as Canada |
| **Reading** | Finland | New Zealand Australia Ireland Japan |
| **Mathematics** | Japan Korea | Finland New Zealand Australia Switzerland United Kingdom |
| **Science** | Japan Korea Finland | New Zealand Australia United Kingdom |

Note: Differences in average scores between two countries are <u>not</u> statistically significant when the confidence interval for the average score for each country overlaps. Countries performing about the same as Canada have a confidence interval for the average score that overlaps with that of Canada.

**FIGURE 1.1**

## Average Scores and Confidence Intervals by Province and Country: READING

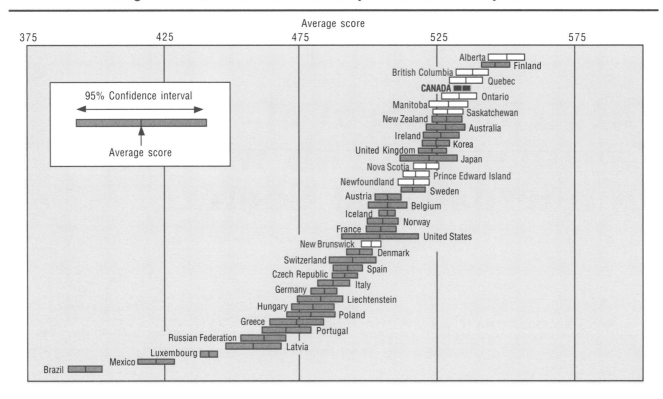

**FIGURE 1.2**

## Average Scores and Confidence Intervals by Province and Country: MATHEMATICS

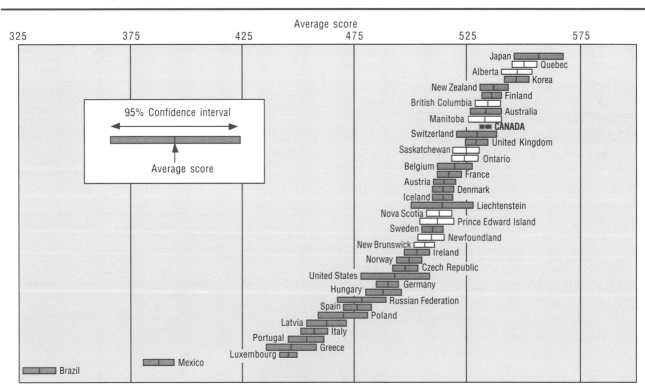

**FIGURE 1.3**

**Average Scores and Confidence Intervals by Province and Country: SCIENCE**

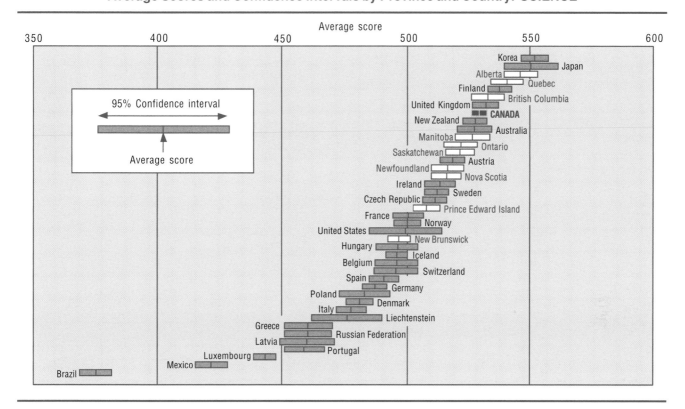

While this was the first time that the PISA tests were administered, this is not the first program to test international achievement. The International Association for the Evaluation of Educational Achievement has conducted a number of such studies over the past twenty years. The most recent of these, the Third International Mathematics and Science Study (TIMSS), administered mathematics and science tests in 1995 and 1999.[3] While the TIMSS and PISA studies are not directly comparable because of differences in frameworks, age differences and differences in some participating countries, it is fair to say that Canada's achievement ranking relative to other countries has improved substantially over time. Canada has risen from a mid-ranked country to one of the top-ranked countries in the 1999 TIMSS, and now in the PISA assessments.

This does not tell us *how much* achievement has actually improved, however, or indeed if it has improved at all. It simply indicates that Canada has advanced in relation to other countries. Successive assessments using the same test are needed to examine improvement in absolute terms. Both PISA and the OECD and Statistics Canada adult literacy studies[4] are international assessments that explicitly provide for tracking change

in achievement over time. These studies should enhance our understanding of the evolution of achievement and the factors underlying observed change.

### A note on statistical comparisons

The performance of students in different countries (and within Canada, in different provinces) was compared by looking at the average scores for all students in each country and at the distribution of these scores. For example, the score achieved by the top 10% of students tells us something about how the best students in each country are performing.

Because the available scores were based on samples of students from each country, we cannot say with certainty that these scores are the same as those that would have been obtained had all 15-year-old students been tested. We use a statistic called the *standard error* to express the degree of uncertainty in the scores for the sample compared with the population. Using the standard error, we can construct a *confidence interval*, which is a range of scores within which we can say, with a known probability (such as 95%), that the score for the full population is likely to fall. The 95% confidence interval used in this report represents a range of plus or minus about two standard errors around the average.

When comparing scores among countries or provinces, we must consider the degree of error in each score before we can say that two scores are significantly different from each other. Standard errors and confidence intervals may be used as the basis for performing these comparative statistical tests. Such tests allow us to say, with a known probability, whether there are actual differences in the populations being compared. For example, when we report that an observed difference is *significant at the .05 level*, we are saying that the probability is less than .05 that the observed difference could have occurred because of sampling error. When comparing countries and provinces, extensive use is made of this type of test to reduce the likelihood that differences due to sampling errors will be overstated.

Only statistically significant differences are noted as *significant* in this report.

# Provincial results in an international context

Most provinces performed well in reading, science and mathematics. In fact, the majority of provinces performed as well as the top ranked countries in the world (Figures 1.1 to 1.3). The performance of students in Alberta was significantly above the Canadian average in all three domains, as was the performance of Quebec students in mathematics and science. In Ontario, Manitoba, Saskatchewan and British Columbia, the performance of students was about the same as the Canadian average in all three domains while the performance of students in Newfoundland, Prince Edward Island, Nova Scotia and New Brunswick was significantly lower. The performance of students in the four Atlantic Provinces was, however, at or above the middle of the international range.

## FIGURE 1.4

### Average Scores and Confidence Intervals for Provinces and Countries: READING RETRIEVING

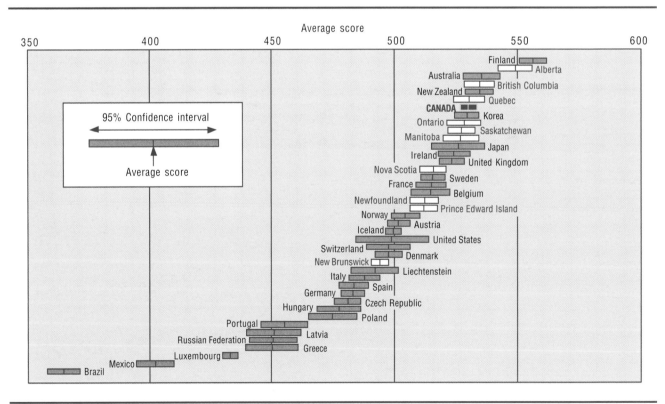

**FIGURE 1.5**

## Average Scores and Confidence Intervals for Provinces and Countries: READING REFLECTING

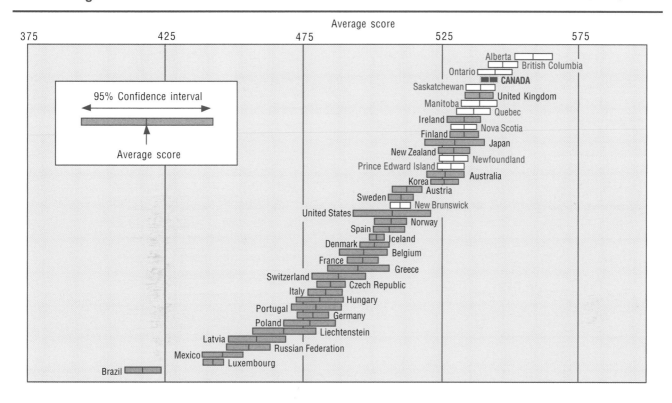

**FIGURE 1.6**

## Average Scores and Confidence Intervals for Provinces and Countries: READING INTERPRETING

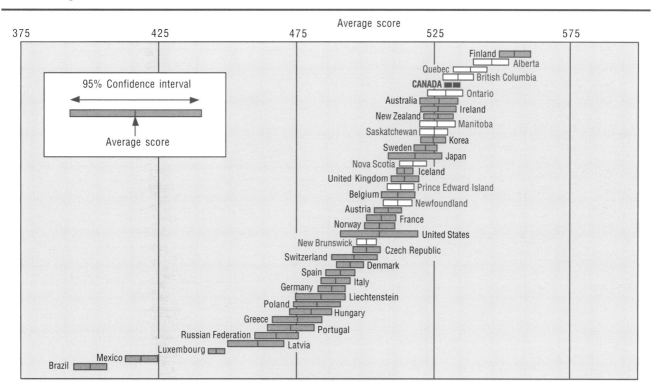

Results for reading achievement are also presented for three sub-scales measuring different reading competencies: retrieving, interpreting and reflecting (Figures 1.4 to 1.6). Interestingly, Canada's performance on the reading reflecting sub-scale was significantly above that of Finland. Definitions of the reading sub-scales are presented in Annex B: Definitions of Key Variables and Constructs.

The rankings observed in the PISA data agree, generally, with those drawn from other sources. Within Canada, the School Achievement Indicators Program (SAIP) has administered reading and writing, mathematics and science tests to 13-year-olds and 16-year-olds in all provinces and territories on a rotating basis since 1993.[5] These assessments reveal small but persistent differences between jurisdictions, with students in British Columbia, the Prairie provinces and Quebec tending to do better than those in Ontario and the Atlantic provinces. A similar pattern has emerged in TIMSS (although not all provinces were sampled adequately in TIMSS to give a full set of provincial comparisons).

---

### Comparing Canadian results to those of selected countries

For all Canadian provinces, the samples were large enough to allow the results to be compared with those of other provinces and countries. To simplify the presentation of Canadian results, all of the analysis in this chapter that extends beyond an examination of average performance, and all of the analyses in the remaining chapters, will be based on a subset of countries. Thirteen countries were selected for comparison with Canada and the provinces. In addition to other G8 countries (France, Germany, Italy, Japan, United Kingdom, United States and the Russian Federation), Australia, Belgium, Finland, Mexico, Sweden and Switzerland were selected because of their similarities to Canada, their record of high achievement or their relevance to Canada. An analysis of the performance of all countries is presented in the international OECD report, *Knowledge and Skills for Life – First results from the OECD Programme for International Student Assessment.*

In addition to the tables and figures presented within the body of this and subsequent chapters, results are also presented in a series of detailed tables in Annex A: Tables.

---

# The distribution of scores

We can learn more about how students perform by looking at how the scores are distributed within each country or province. Two countries with the same average may have quite different numbers of especially high- or low-performing students. Differences in how the scores are distributed tell us something about the degree of equality in proficiency among students within a country and across countries.

For example, the distribution of reading scores in Canada, Finland, and the United States is presented in Figure 1.7. Although there are significant differences in the average scores of these countries, the largest peak, or most frequent score, in each country is fairly similar. When examining the distribution of scores to the right of the peaks, it is clear that the distribution for Canada is similar to that of Finland across a wide range. This indicates that Canada's highest performing students performed as well as the highest performing Finnish students. In contrast, only the very highest performing students in the United States appear to have performed as well as those in either Canada or Finland. When looking at the distribution to the left of the peak, Finland had fewer low-performing students than did Canada. The United States, however, had more lower performing students than either Canada or Finland. In the distribution of scores for the United States there are two peaks. The first, smaller peak represents a large sub-population of students that performed less well than those represented by the second, larger peak. It is the influence of this sub-population that caused the average score for the United States to fall well below that of Canada and Finland.

A simpler way to examine distributions is to calculate the *percentile scores*—the scores below which a specified percentage of students are found. This gives us percentile ranks, or just *percentiles.* Thus, the 10th percentile is the one below which we find 10% of students. The 50th percentile is called the median and is the score below which we find half the students. By comparing scores at specific percentiles, we are able to examine the distribution of scores within a population. Tables 1.7 to 1.9, presented in Annex A, show the scores that correspond to the 5th, 10th, 25th, 50th, 75th, 90th and 95th percentiles for reading, mathematics and science for Canada as a whole, the provinces and selected countries.

Returning to the examination of reading performance in Canada, the United States and Finland, the score for the 95th percentile was identical in Finland and Canada. In the United States, the score, while appearing to be lower, was not significantly different from that of Canada or Finland. Canada's score for the 5th percentile, however, was significantly below that of Finland and the score for the United States was significantly below that of both Canada and Finland.

Belgium is perhaps the best example of how spread out scores can be toward the low end of the distribution. In all three sets of scores, the 5th percentile score in Belgium is among the lowest of all countries even though the average score places the country at a fairly high rank. As a final example, although Canada and Australia have similar average scores, Australia's distribution is somewhat broader than Canada's, indicating a more diverse population. Most provinces have fairly narrow distributions compared with other countries.

## Variation in proficiency

A measure of the distribution of scores within and across countries is obtained by examining the ratio of scores at the 90th percentile to that at the 10th percentile. A ratio close to 1 indicates that all students in a country achieve nearly the same level. Higher ratios indicate relatively greater variation.

Jurisdictions with high average scores tend to have less variation in achievement than do those with low average scores (Figures 1.8 to 1.10). However, when we rank countries according to this index, Canada's rank shifts down slightly. This indicates that, despite high overall performance, relatively more students in Canada are near both the top and the bottom of the distribution than in some other highly-ranked countries, such as Finland and Japan.

At the same time, there are differences among provinces in the inequality index. Generally speaking, provinces that performed better also tended to have less variation between the top and bottom of the distribution.

---

### FIGURE 1.7

**The Distribution of Reading Scores in Canada, Finland and the United States**

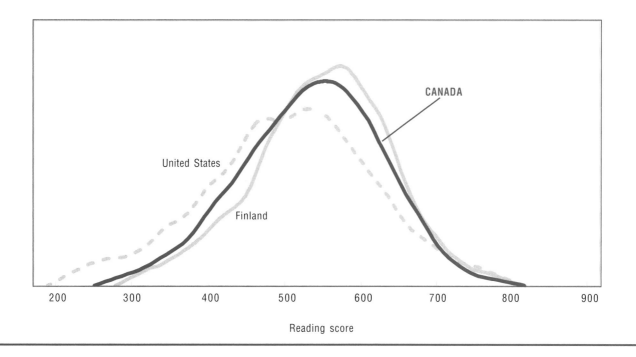

Reading score

---

## FIGURE 1.8

### Inequality Index of Reading Scores (90th percentile/10th percentile)

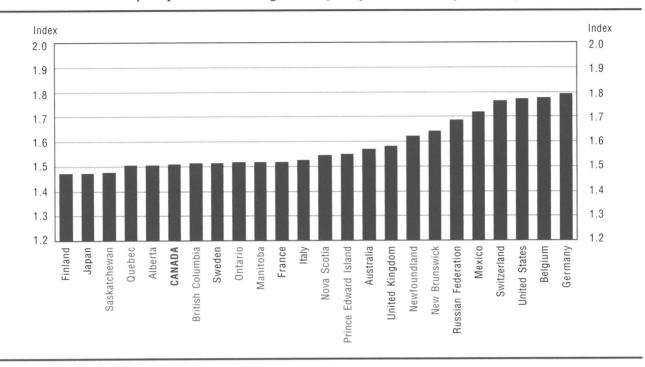

## FIGURE 1.9

### Inequality Index of Mathematics Scores (90th percentile/10th percentile)

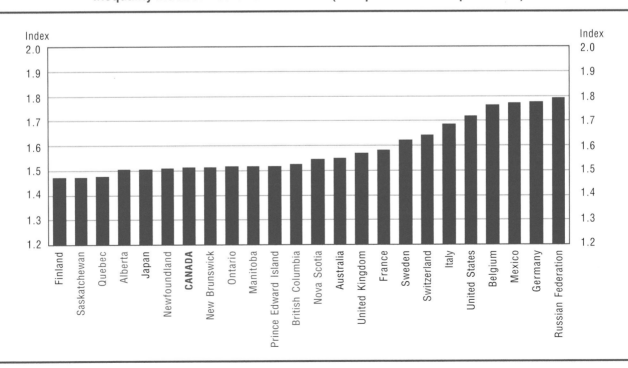

**FIGURE 1.10**

### Inequality Index of Science Scores (90th percentile/10th percentile)

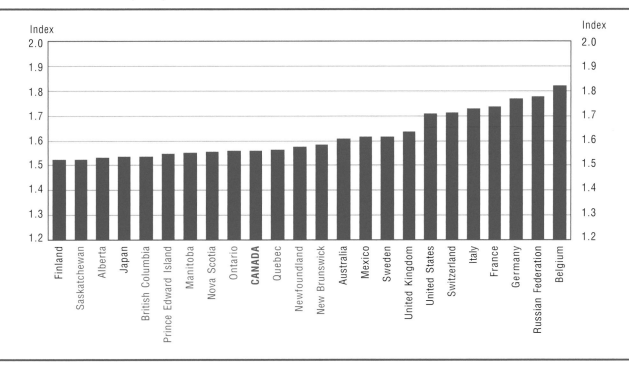

# Distribution of high performers

An argument can be made that individuals who can achieve at the highest possible levels make an important contribution to the well being of a society in an increasingly competitive global economy. For example, they may be most likely to contribute to our ability to undertake world-class research and development in the future.

Another way to compare jurisdictions is to compare the proportion of students performing at the highest levels. This can be done by examining the performance of all of the students in the 13 selected countries and in Canada, and finding the scores for this international group that correspond to selected percentile ranks, such as the 90th percentile (top 10% of students), the 75% percentile (top 25% of students) and the 50th percentile (top 50% of students). The percentage of students in each jurisdiction with scores equal to or above these international ranks is presented in Figures 1.11 to 1.13.

Again, this perspective reveals a somewhat different pattern than the others. In particular, the differences between jurisdictions in the percentage of students at the very top of the score distribution (top 10%) are much larger than the differences in overall averages. For mathematics and science, many provinces have shifted lower in the international rankings, and the differences among provinces are more pronounced.

# Reading skill levels

Rankings can tell us how countries and provinces compare with each other overall. Rankings tell us nothing, however, about what students can actually do. We can elicit more information from the data if we are able to describe what can be done at specific score levels. For this reason, reading achievement was divided into five levels.

As expected, the highest-ranking jurisdictions overall also tend to have the highest proportion of students at Level 5 (Figure 1.14). However, a few substantial shifts are apparent. For example, Japan has relatively few Level 5 students, although with a large proportion at Level 4 it has a high ranking on overall performance. On the other hand, Australia ranks higher on this scale than on the overall performance scale, because of a relatively high proportion of students at Level 5. Generally speaking, the positions of Canada and the provinces do not shift much.

**FIGURE 1.11**

## Percent of Students Above 90th, 75th and 50th International Percentiles: READING

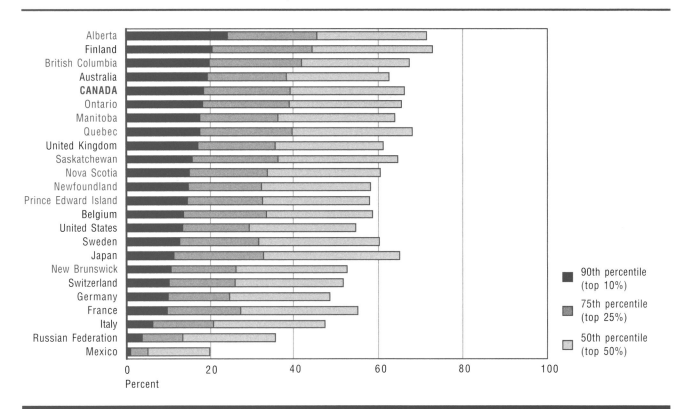

**FIGURE 1.12**

## Percent of Students Above 90th, 75th and 50th International Percentiles: MATHEMATICS

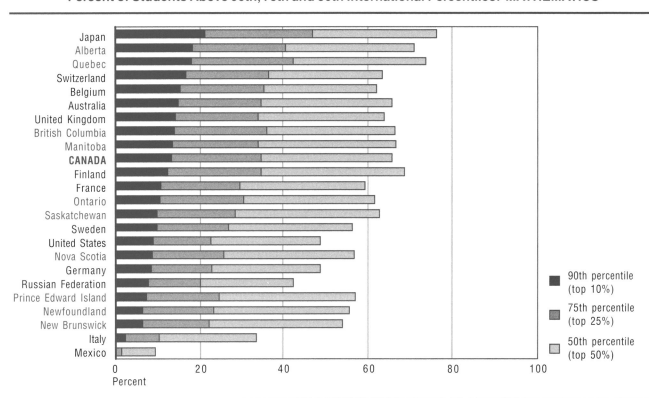

**FIGURE 1.13**

## Percent of Students Above 90th, 75th and 50th International Percentiles: Science

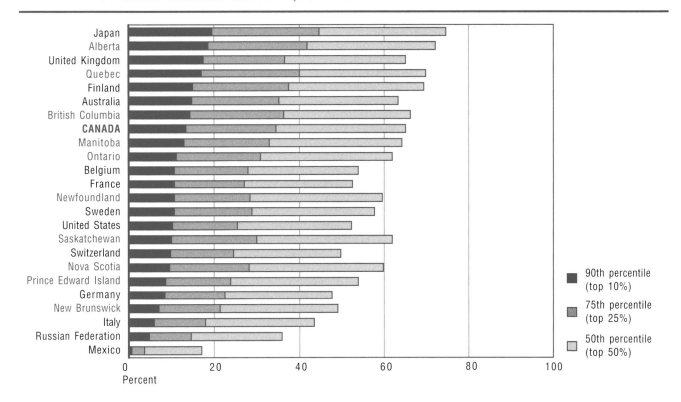

**FIGURE 1.14**

## Reading Proficiency Scales: Percent of Students at Each Level

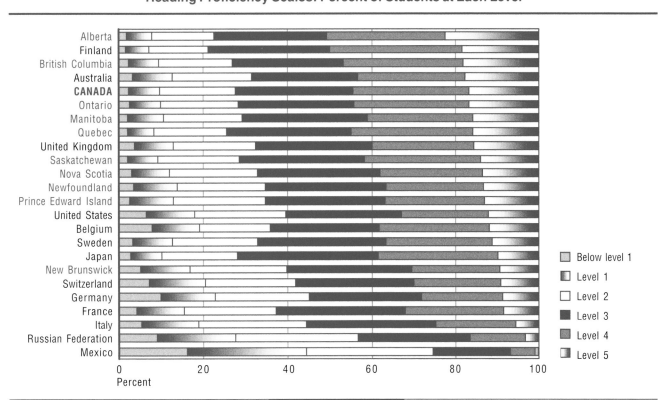

## Five levels of reading literacy

Reading achievement was divided into five levels. Essentially, these levels represent the most difficult test items that a student could answer. Therefore, a student at one level could be assumed to be able to answer questions at all lower levels. To help in interpretation, these levels were linked to specific score ranges on the original scale. Because the five levels are complex to describe, an example from each level is given for the *reading retrieving scale*. Tasks of similar complexity were required for each level of the other reading scales.

### Level 1 (score from 335 to 407)

Students were shown a notice from a personnel department about a service that would help with job mobility. They were asked to find a single explicitly stated piece of information—how to find out more about the service—which was signalled by a heading in the text that matched the term used in the question.

### Level 2 (score from 408 to 480)

Students were required to state how to check that a bicycle seat was in the right position, by finding two pieces of connected information in an assembly manual. The placement of the relevant information was clearly stated in the question.

### Level 3 (score from 481 to 552)

Looking at a complex international airline timetable, with prominent competing information, students had to find a single piece of information that satisfied three conditions—time, destination and connecting city. For information about one of the conditions, the reader had to refer to a separate list of abbreviations.

### Level 4 (score from 553 to 626)

Presented with a relatively long, dense extract from a play, students had to use information embedded in a stage direction in order to mark the positions of two actors on a diagram of the stage.

### Level 5 (score above 626)

Students were given a complex and unfamiliar set of instructions about how to make telephone calls from a hotel room, and a letter with the phone number of a friend in a different country. They were required to find and organise in correct sequence four pieces of information and to draw inferences to work out exactly how to dial the number.

## Performance below level 1

Students performing below Level 1 (total reading score below 335) are not able to routinely show the most basic type of knowledge and skills that PISA seeks to measure. Such students have serious difficulties in using reading literacy as a tool to advance their knowledge and skills in other areas. Placement at this level does not mean that these students have no literacy skills. Most of these students are able to correctly complete some of the PISA items. Their pattern of responses to the assessment is such that they would be expected to solve less than half of the tasks from a test composed of only level 1 items.

## Interpreting differences in PISA reading scores

A difference of 73 points between two average scores could be thought of as representing about one proficiency level in reading literacy. A difference of one proficiency level can be considered a comparatively large difference in student performance in substantive terms. For example, on the interpreting scale, Level 3 distinguishes students who can typically integrate several parts of a text, understand a relationship or construe the meaning of a word or phrase, and can compare, contrast and categorise competing information according to a range of criteria. At Level 2, students can be expected only to identify the main idea in a text, to understand relationships, make and apply simple categories, and construe meaning within a limited part of a text where information is not prominent but only low-level inferences are required.

# How do boys and girls compare?

All jurisdictions have an interest in reducing gender disparities in educational performance. Previous studies have revealed a pattern of higher performance for girls in reading and writing and for boys in mathematics and science. There has also been a tendency for these disparities to widen as students progress through the education system. In Canada, the SAIP studies have revealed small but significant differences favouring girls in reading and writing but few gender differences in mathematics and science achievement.

In PISA, girls performed significantly better than boys on the reading test in all countries and in all provinces (Table 1.17). In contrast, for mathematics and science, few significant differences between girls and boys were observed (Tables 1.18 and 1.19). This does not indicate that there are, necessarily, few differences between the genders in mathematics and science, only that as minor domains in PISA 2000 differences were not observable.

Canada, France and Germany were the only countries where small gender differences in mathematics achievement were significant. In these countries, results favoured boys, however, the difference in average scores between the genders was much less than that observed for reading. With the smaller sample sizes in individual provinces, and consequent higher standard errors, the small differences between the genders in mathematics were not significant in any individual province. For science achievement, there were no significant differences between girls and boys in any country or province.

## Achievement of Canadian students by language of the school system

This section examines the performance of students in English and French school systems for the five Canadian provinces that sampled these population groups separately.[6] The focus is on the performance of the minority group (students in francophone school systems in Nova Scotia, New Brunswick, Ontario and Manitoba, and students in the anglophone school system in Quebec) relative to the majority.[7]

The SAIP assessment gives the only available historical data on the performance of the two linguistic groups. In general, students from francophone school systems outside of Quebec performed at levels below the Canadian average, below their counterparts in Quebec, and below the levels of the anglophone majorities in the same provinces. There are a few exceptions to this, including the relatively high performance of the francophone education system in Nova Scotia on the 1997 mathematics assessment. Within Quebec, the performance of the two linguistic groups has historically been similar and relatively high.

A comparison of PISA results within each province is given in Table 1.20. In all provinces except Quebec, students enrolled in minority language education systems performed at a significantly lower level in reading than did students in the majority systems in the same provinces. In mathematics, only Ontario had significant differences

among the two school systems, with results favouring the anglophone system. For science, there were significant differences favouring the anglophone system in Nova Scotia, New Brunswick, Ontario and Manitoba.

In Quebec, the differences between the two school systems were not significant for any of the subjects. In addition, Quebec students performed well relative to those in other provinces with significant linguistic minorities.

Further analysis of the information collected through PISA and YITS will clarify the extent to which important background variables, such as the main language spoken at home, contribute to these differences and will explore the role schools play in amplifying or attenuating these differences.

## Conclusion

Reading is key to many other areas of activity, both inside and outside school. While the cumulative effect of poor reading performance is not fully understood, it is clear from the International Adult Literacy Survey (IALS) that adults with low levels of literacy skills are at a significant disadvantage in Canada's labour market.[8] As a result, while Canada's overall performance in PISA was very good, the existence of disparities among provinces, and between official language groups within some provinces, is a matter of concern and merits further analysis.

The lower performance levels for boys in reading will also concern policy makers both in Canada and in other countries. Further analysis, presented in the next chapter, points to differences in key individual characteristics, such as enjoyment of reading. A smaller difference, favouring boys, in mathematics achievement was also observed at the Canada level. The results of PISA 2003, where mathematics will be the major domain, should clarify the extent to which gender differences in mathematics occur among jurisdictions.

While the comparative approach taken in this chapter does not lend itself to developing explanations for these disparities, the overall PISA/YITS study, along with data available from SAIP, IALS and other large-scale assessments, provides, for the first time, a series of rich databases that should allow researchers and educators to explore how resources, schools and classroom conditions—as well as individual and family circumstances—affect variation in achievement. Subsequent chapters of this report give a preliminary analysis of some of these factors and provide an indication of the potential for more comprehensive analysis.

# Notes

1. Results for the Netherlands are not presented due to a low response rate. As a result, only 31 countries are included in Figures 1.1 to 1.6.

2. The performance of students was expressed as a number of points on a scale constructed so that the average score for students in all participating OECD countries was 500 and its standard deviation was 100. This means that about two-thirds of students internationally scored between 400 and 600 on the scale.

3. For more information on TIMSS consult the website www.timss.bc.edu.

4. The OECD and Statistics Canada International Adult Literacy Survey (IALS) and the forthcoming International Adult Literacy and Life Skills Survey (ALL).

5. For more information on SAIP consult the website www.cmec.ca.

6. The number of participating students in the francophone and anglophone school systems were, respectively: Nova Scotia (216; 2714), New Brunswick (1150;1813), Quebec (3150;1347), Ontario (1003;3287), and Manitoba (241;2358).

7. Within all anglophone school systems, both students in French Immersion programs and those in regular programs completed the reading test in English. Some French Immersion students completed the mathematics and science tests in French.

8. OECD and Statistics Canada (2000), *Literacy in the Information Age: Final Report of the OECD Literacy Study,* OECD and Minister of Industry, Paris and Ottawa.

# Chapter 2

# The Impact of Individual Characteristics on Achievement

T his chapter presents an analysis of how the personal characteristics of individual students measured in the PISA study influence their achievement in reading, mathematics and science. Child-centred learning theory holds that since individual learners have the most direct responsibility for their academic outcomes, their unique characteristics play an important role in the educational process.[1]

This chapter examines the effects on student achievement of a number of individual characteristics of youth including reading behaviours, attitudes toward school, career and education expectations, and employment experiences. The first part of the chapter examines the absolute effects of individual characteristics on achievement. The second part analyses these individual characteristics within a multifaceted framework that accounts for interrelationships among the variables. This analysis of relative effects allows us to discern which variables have the strongest relationships with achievement.

### Estimating absolute and relative effects

Chapters 2, 3 and 4 present the *absolute* and *relative* effects of individual, family and school characteristics on student achievement. The absolute effect refers to the variable's effect in the absence of other variables— it measures the independent contribution of the variable to student achievement.[2] The relative effect refers to the variable's effect in the presence of other variables—it measures the residual contribution of the variable to student achievement. A variable may be important by itself but unimportant when other variables are also taken into consideration. To estimate relative effects, variables are entered together into one multiple regression model for each country and province.

The following thresholds in the absolute values of the effect size statistic were used to judge the magnitude of the effect:

Trivial:     Less than $|0.10|$

Small:      Between $|0.10|$ and $|0.30|$

Moderate:  Between $|0.30|$ and $|0.50|$

Large:      Greater than $|0.50|$

An effect size less than $|0.10|$ indicates that less than 1% of the variance in achievement scores is explained by the variable and, as such, reflects a trivial impact.

For more information on standardised effects see the notes accompanying the tables in Annex A.

# Reading behaviours

*Reading enjoyment* had a positive effect on reading achievement in all countries, with a higher level of reading enjoyment associated with a higher level of achievement (Table 2.1). In almost all countries, the effects of reading enjoyment were moderate. Canada was among the countries where the effect was the greatest. Within Canada, a moderate positive effect of reading enjoyment on reading achievement was evident in all provinces.

As with many of the individual characteristics examined in this chapter, the relationship between the characteristic and performance may be interpreted in two ways. In this case, reading enjoyment may improve reading skills, while better readers may enjoy reading more.

*Reading diversity*, that is reading a variety of different types of material for enjoyment, was positively associated with reading achievement (Table 2.1). The effects were small or moderate in almost all countries. Within Canada, small positive effects of reading diversity on reading achievement were evident in all provinces except Nova Scotia and New Brunswick, where moderate positive effects were found.

Students were asked to report their *daily time spent reading for enjoyment*. Overall, in all countries and provinces, reading performance increased as the time spent reading for enjoyment grew (Table 2.2). There was, however, no added benefit of reading more than one or two hours daily in most countries and provinces. In Canada and Germany, (and also in New Brunswick, Saskatchewan and British Columbia), students reading two or more hours daily had significantly lower average achievement scores than those reading one to two hours daily. This phenomenon may result because these students read more slowly and thus take more time to read. Further analysis is required to understand this relationship.

*The use of public and school libraries* measures the frequency with which students borrow books from libraries to read for enjoyment. In all countries, except Mexico, and in all provinces there was a significant difference in reading achievement between those who borrowed books once per month and/or several times per month and those who never borrowed books (Table 2.3).[3] The same pattern was observed in countries and provinces for science achievement, with only students in France, Mexico and the Russian Federation not showing benefits of library use. In Mathematics,

differences in average achievement between those using libraries and those never using libraries were significant in all countries except France, the United States, Italy, the Russian Federation and Mexico. Among provinces, these differences were significant for mathematics in all provinces except Newfoundland, New Brunswick and Alberta.

# Attitudes toward school

Student attitudes toward school were measured through time spent on homework and a measure of the sense of belonging to school.

*Time spent on homework* had a small or moderate positive effect on achievement in almost all countries and in all provinces (Table 2.4). Among provinces, the only exception was Newfoundland where effects for mathematics and science were trivial. *Sense of belonging to school* did not appear to be related to achievement in most countries and in all provinces (Table 2.4). Where it did have an impact, the effect was small.

# Student career expectations

*Student career expectations*, based on the occupational status of the job students expect to have when they are about thirty, were positively linked to achievement in all countries (Table 2.5). While career aspirations may motivate students to perform better, aspirations may also be influenced by role models, particularly parents, by previous academic performance and by the orientation of students' educational programs.

The effects of student career expectations were small to moderate. Effects were small in six countries, including Canada, in reading; in seven countries, including Canada, in mathematics; and in five countries, including Canada, in science. Other countries had moderate effects. Among provinces, effects were small for all three domains with the exception of Saskatchewan where the effect for reading achievement was moderate.

# Student education expectations

The Youth in Transition Survey (YITS) asked students to specify the highest level of education they expected to achieve. As with career expectations, *student expectations of the highest level of education* had a positive relationship with achievement across all provinces (Table 2.6). The interpretation of this relationship, however, is complex. While the intention to pursue a postsecondary education may motivate students to perform better, students with a record of previous academic success will be the most likely to aspire to higher levels of education. Also, students' educational aspirations will be linked to the orientation of their educational programs and to their parents' educational attainment and aspirations for them.

## Working while studying

Using YITS data, a preliminary analysis was undertaken to investigate how working while studying relates to achievement. Table 2.7 presents the average reading, mathematics and science achievement of *students with and without a job in the school year*. In all provinces, students without jobs during the school year had significantly higher average reading performance than did working students. Many provinces did not, however, have significant differences favouring non-working students in mathematics achievement or science achievement.

Nonetheless, for all three domains, as the hours worked per week increased, performance tended to decline. Small negative effects related to the hours worked during weekends and during the school week were found in all provinces for reading, mathematics and science achievement (Table 2.8).

Previous studies have shown that working a limited number of hours while in school does not increase the probability of dropping out of high school.[4] The longer-term impact of combining work and study at age 15 on education and labour-market outcomes will be clarified through future research that takes advantage of the longitudinal nature of YITS.

## The relative importance of individual factors in explaining achievement

Most of the individual characteristics of youth, when considered alone, are significant predictors of student achievement across countries and provinces. Many of these factors, however, are inter-related. Altogether, which of these factors are the most influential, and are there jurisdictional differences? To answer these questions, most of the individual factors examined in this chapter were considered together in one multiple regression model for each country and province.

In addition to the variables previously analysed in this chapter, this analysis includes *Gender*, presented in Chapter 1. Variables from YITS that were included earlier in this chapter, employment experiences and education expectations, are not included in this analysis as they are not available for international comparison.

Table 2.9 presents results of this multiple regression analysis. It shows the magnitude of the relative impact of the variables as small (s), medium (m), or large (l), using the criteria outlined earlier in this chapter. Variables with a negative effect are indicated with a "-" sign.

When all individual characteristics are considered, *reading enjoyment* and *student career expectations* remain important individual characteristics in almost all countries and in all provinces. Reading enjoyment is a predictor of achievement in all countries except Mexico (for all three domains) and France and Japan (for mathematics). Similarly, student career expectations is a significant predictor in all jurisdictions except in Japan for science.

Other reading behaviours, reading diversity and time spent reading for enjoyment, were correlated with reading enjoyment and thus did not emerge as predictors in this analysis in many countries and in most provinces.

In this analysis, gender differences no longer had an effect on reading achievement in all countries except Australia, Finland and Mexico, and in all provinces. This is because the variation in reading achievement between boys and girls is related to differences in reading behaviours between the genders, particularly reading enjoyment, which were included in this analysis. Small effects favouring males in mathematics were apparent in all countries, except Australia and Mexico, and in all provinces. Similarly, in eight countries, including Canada, and in all provinces except New Brunswick, there were small effects favouring males in science.

The PISA 2000 assessment focused on reading achievement and did not gather information that would help us to understand whether or not gender differences are related to differences in enjoyment of mathematics and science or to differences in behaviours that may enhance mathematical or scientific literacy. A more comprehensive analysis of gender differences in mathematics and science will be possible following the administration of PISA in 2003 and 2006.

In a number of provinces and countries (including Canada for reading) the frequency of borrowing books to read for enjoyment from school and public libraries showed a small negative relationship to student achievement. This counter intuitive outcome likely results because this analysis excludes variables measuring family socio-economic background and controls for the effect of other reading behaviours. Among students who enjoy reading for pleasure, those using libraries may have fewer resources with which to purchase reading material. The impact of family socio-economic background on achievement is explored in detail in the next chapter.

Other individual variables showed effects less consistently across countries and provinces. When effects were present, they were small.

## Conclusion

Analysed individually, most factors included in this chapter showed a measurable relationship to achievement. In particular, reading behaviours such as reading enjoyment, reading diversity and time spent reading for enjoyment had strong effects on reading, mathematics and science results. Similarly, time spent on homework showed a small effect on performance. Students' education and career expectations were correlated with performance. For many variables, and most particularly for career and education expectations, the relationship between the variable and achievement may result from complex causes. While individual behaviours may lead to improvements in academic performance, in many cases, the behaviours themselves, such as career aspirations, may result from a student's own evaluation of his or her academic abilities.

Moreover, many of the individual factors analysed in this chapter are correlated. Once these interrelationships were taken into account, only reading enjoyment and career expectations stood out as strongly related to achievement in all three domains. Gender differences in mathematics and science, which are also important factors, merit more comprehensive analysis following future cycles of PISA.

## Notes

1. Miller, John P. and Wayne Seller (1990), *Curriculum: Perspectives and Practices*, Copp Clark Pitman, Toronto.

2. If the variable examined was categorical, average achievement scores were calculated for each category and then compared. If the variable was continuous, regression analysis was performed and an effect size was used to examine the effects of the variable on achievement.

3. In the relative effects analysis, the relationship between the use of libraries and achievement is negative in many jurisdictions. This outcome is likely due to the close relationship between this behaviour and family socio-economic status which becomes evident once effects of other reading behaviours have been accounted for.

4. Dagenais, Marcel, Claude Montmarquette, Daniel Parent, Benoit Durocher and François Raymond (1999), *Working While Studying and School Leavers: Causes, Consequences and Policy Interventions.* Applied Research Branch Research Papers Series, Human Resources Development Canada catalogue R-99-5E, Ottawa.

   Sunter, Deborah (1993), "School, Work and Dropping Out", *Perspectives on Labour and Income*, Statistics Canada catalogue no. 75-001, Summer, pp. 44-52, Ottawa.

# Chapter 3

# The Impact of Family Characteristics and Home Environment on Achievement

A student's family and home environment influences achievement. This chapter identifies a set of variables that describe these characteristics and examines their relationship to student achievement in reading, mathematics and science.

This chapter examines the effects on student achievement of a variety of family factors, including family background, home environment, family educational support, parental involvement and parental expectations. The first part of the chapter examines the absolute effects of family characteristics on achievement. The second part analyses these characteristics within a multifaceted framework that accounts for interrelationships among the variables. This analysis of relative effects allows us to discern which variables have the strongest relationships with achievement.[1]

## Family background

Family background characteristics which were examined include family structure, the number of siblings in the family and family socio-economic status. *Family structure* divides students into two categories: those in single-parent families and those in two-parent families. In half of the 14 countries examined, including Canada, students from two-parent families had significantly higher levels of achievement than did students from single-parent families (Table 3.1). Differences in student performance resulting from family structure were, however, linked to differences in other important characteristics, particularly family socio-economic status. The interrelationship among family characteristics is explored later in this chapter.

Among provinces, the average reading performance of students in two-parent families was significantly above that of students in one-parent families in New Brunswick, Manitoba, Saskatchewan, Alberta and British Columbia. In mathematics, there was a significant difference in New Brunswick, Quebec, Manitoba, Saskatchewan, and Alberta and in science, the advantage was significant in New Brunswick, Manitoba and Alberta.

In many countries, a larger *number of siblings* in the family had a small negative relationship with student achievement in all three domains (Table 3.2). In Canada, there was a small negative effect of the number of siblings on mathematics and science achievement. For reading achievement, effects in Canada were trivial. In Japan and Finland, effects were trivial across all three domains.

The number of siblings in the family had a negative relationship with achievement in some provinces. In Manitoba, Saskatchewan and Alberta, there was a small negative effect present in all three domains. There was also a small negative effect on mathematics achievement in Quebec, Manitoba, Saskatchewan, Alberta and British

Columbia, and on science achievement in all provinces except Prince Edward Island, Nova Scotia and New Brunswick.

*Socio-economic differences* in academic achievement have been abundantly documented in major national and international studies. In this chapter, socio-economic status (SES) is derived from student responses regarding parental occupations. In all countries examined, students with higher family socio-economic statuses had higher achievement than did students with lower family socio-economic statuses. Almost all countries and provinces exhibited small or moderate effects of family socio-economic status on student performance in all three domains (Table 3.3).

Socio-economic impacts on academic achievement are often expressed in the research literature as socio-economic gradients. These gradients are measures of the extent to which inequalities in academic achievement exist within a population (e.g., among students in a country or in a province) as a result of socio-economic status. The slope of the gradient is an indication of the extent of inequality attributable to socio-economic factors. Steeper gradients indicate a greater relationship between socio-economic status and student performance,

or more inequality; shallower gradients indicate a smaller relationship between socio-economic background and student performance, or less inequality.

Figure 3.1 displays this relationship for reading achievement among G8 countries and Finland.[2] Countries with high average reading achievement also tended to have less variability in scores across socio-economic groups. Canada had both a shallow socio-economic gradient and high scores across socio-economic groups. Germany, on the other hand, had the steepest gradient, indicating the greatest variation in student reading performance across socio-economic groups.

The relationship between socio-economic status and achievement can also be examined by comparing average scores of students from families with the highest socio-economic statuses with the average scores of students from families with the lowest socio-economic statuses (Table 3.4). Among the fourteen countries included in this analysis, Canada, along with Finland and Japan, exhibited far less variation in reading scores between these two groups than did most other countries. Results were similar for mathematics and science achievement. This suggests that achievement scores are

**FIGURE 3.1**

**Socio-economic Gradients of G8 Countries and Finland, READING**

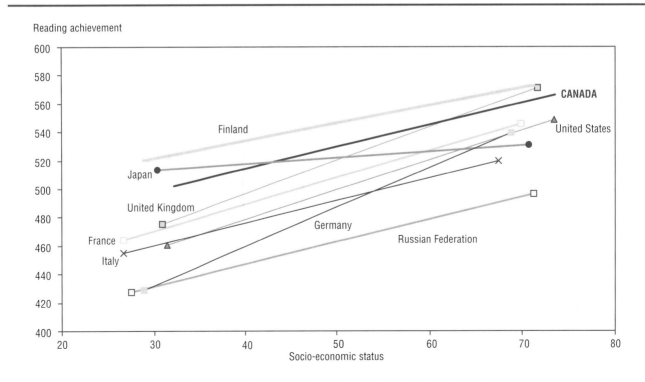

more equivalent among students with different socio-economic backgrounds in Canada, than they are in many other countries.

Within Canada, students from Saskatchewan exhibited less variation in reading, mathematics and science achievement by family socio-economic background than did students in other provinces. Performance of students with mid-to-high socio-economic backgrounds in this province, however, fell below that of several other provinces.

Alberta, on the other hand, had the highest achievement scores across all levels of family socio-economic background in both reading and science. Similarly, Quebec had the highest scores across all levels of family socio-economic status in mathematics. In Alberta and Quebec, however, there was greater variation in achievement across socio-economic groups, than in Saskatchewan.

Newfoundland had the greatest variation in achievement scores across socio-economic groups in both reading and science, while Nova Scotia had the greatest variation in mathematics.

# Home environment

Family possessions, home educational resources, number of books at home, home cultural possessions and cultural activities are used as indicators of home environment. While the independent effect of each of these factors is explored, many of these variables are related to parental socio-economic status. The interrelationship among all family characteristics is discussed later in this chapter.

*Family possessions* is measured by material possessions in the home. Family possessions had a small positive effect on achievement in almost all countries, including Canada, and in most provinces (Table 3.5). Thus, a higher level of family possessions was associated with a higher level of achievement in reading, mathematics and science.

The variable *home educational resources* describes the extent to which families facilitate student learning by providing educational necessities such as a desk, a calculator, a dictionary and a quiet place to study. A higher level of home educational resources is associated with a higher level of achievement in all 14 countries. The effect of home educational resources on performance in reading, mathematics and science was moderate in

the United States, Belgium and Mexico and small in the remaining countries and Canadian provinces. (Table 3.5).

*Home cultural possessions* refer to a family's cultural environment—having classic literature, books of poetry and works of art in the home. Home cultural possessions had moderate positive effects on reading achievement in seven countries, on mathematics achievement in two countries and on science achievement in four countries (Table 3.5). Small positive effects occurred in Canada and in the remaining countries and in all provinces across all three domains. Among countries and provinces, the effects of home cultural possessions on achievement were larger for reading achievement than they were for mathematics.

The variable *students' cultural activities* measures the frequency with which students take part in cultural activities such as visiting museums, going to concerts and watching live theatre. Cultural activities had a positive effect on academic achievement in all countries, with a higher level of cultural activities associated with a higher level of achievement (Table 3.5). Small positive effects of cultural activities were found in many countries, while moderate effects were found in the United Kingdom, Germany, Belgium and Mexico for reading; in Belgium for mathematics; and in Belgium and Mexico for science. Within Canada, the effects of cultural activities were small in all provinces, except Newfoundland and Prince Edward Island, where effects for reading were moderate. As with home cultural possessions, effects of cultural activities tended to be larger for reading achievement than for mathematics achievement.

In addition to the presence of resources at home to assist their education, students reported an estimate of the total *number of books in their home*. Across countries and Canadian provinces, average student achievement in all three domains increased with the number of books at home (Table 3.6).

# Family educational support

*Family educational support* measures the extent to which immediate family members (mothers, fathers and siblings) help students with their schoolwork. Family educational support was negatively associated with achievement in almost all countries (Table 3.7). This indicates that students with lower academic achievement, and perhaps greater need for help, tend to receive more help from family members than do students with higher achievement.[3]

Small negative effects of family educational support were found in many countries in all three domains. Within Canada, however, there was little relationship between family educational support and reading performance in all provinces, except Newfoundland and Quebec. For mathematics and science, there were small negative effects of family educational support in most provinces. This may indicate that parents of lower-performing students are taking an active role in their children's education.

## Parental involvement

Parental involvement is reflected by two variables: *parental academic interest* and *parental social interest*. Academic interest is indicated by the extent of cultural input from parents, including discussing books, films and television programs and political and social issues with their children. Social interest is the degree of parent-child socialisation in a family (e.g., eating the evening meal together, discussing schoolwork and spending time talking).

Academic interest was a consistently important family factor with positive effects on achievement in all countries and provinces (Table 3.8). That is, a higher level of parental academic interest was associated with a higher level of achievement. There were small effects found in all countries and provinces, with the exception of Australia where the effect for reading was moderate, and Italy, where the effect for mathematics was trivial. As was the case for some home environment characteristics, effects for reading tended to be larger than those found for mathematics.

Parent social interest had small positive effects on reading achievement in many countries and in all provinces except Quebec. The size of the effects were, however, lower than those found for parental academic interest. Parental social interest had a weaker relationship with achievement in mathematics and science, having small effects in only six countries for mathematics and in eight for science. Among provinces, few had positive effects for mathematics while most did have small positive effects for science.

## Parental expectations

This section examines the relationship between achievement measured by PISA and *parental expectations* related to education. Data for this investigation come from the Canadian Youth in Transition Survey (YITS).

Parents specified expectations for their children in YITS in terms of the highest level of educational achievement they expected their child would achieve. Few parents expected their children not to graduate from high school and thus, the analysis focuses on other categories of parental education expectations (Table 3.9). Across all domains and in all provinces, a universal pattern emerged which linked a higher level of parental expectations with a higher level of student achievement. In all provinces and in all domains, students whose parents expected them to get a university education had significantly higher average performance than did those whose parents expected them to complete a college or trade diploma or a high school diploma. The only exception was in Saskatchewan for mathematics.

In all provinces, except Prince Edward Island and Ontario, the average performance of students in reading was significantly higher for those whose parents expected a college diploma than for those whose parents expected a high school diploma. These differences were significant for both mathematics and science achievement in Nova Scotia, Quebec and Saskatchewan; for mathematics achievement in New Brunswick; and for science achievement in Alberta.

Differences in performance for students whose parents expected them to complete a trade diploma and for those whose parents expected a high school diploma were not significant in most provinces. Only Quebec had significant differences across all three domains, while New Brunswick had significant differences in reading and Saskatchewan in science.

As with students' own education expectations, presented in Chapter 2, the relationship between expectations and performance is complex. Parental expectations may influence a student's own educational hopes and academic success. A parent's expectations, however, may also be influenced by how well their child is performing academically, the orientation of their child's educational program, and their knowledge of their child's own preferences.

# The relative importance of family factors in explaining achievement

Although all of the family and home factors considered in this chapter are related to student achievement when considered individually, many are also closely related to each other. To determine which of the factors exerts the strongest influence on achievement and the extent to which there are jurisdictional differences, all family and home factors examined in this chapter were considered together in a multiple regression model for each country and province.

In addition to the variables previously discussed in this chapter, this analysis included a variable, *language spoken at home,* which distinguished students who were not born in Canada and who spoke a language other than English and French in their home from other students. In the case of other countries, the variable looked at those students who were foreign-born and spoke a language at home other than a national language or dialect. This variable was included with family factors since it does not provide a measure of a student's own fluency in either French or English, but a measure of a student's home environment. It was not analysed individually for absolute effects because of small sample sizes for this group. The variable was included in the multiple regression, however, because it is of considerable interest as a family factor. At the same time, the YITS variable *parent's education expectations* was not included in this analysis as it is not available for international comparison.

Table 3.10 presents results of this multiple regression analysis. It shows the magnitude of the relative impact of the variables as small (s), medium (m), or large (l), using the criteria outlined in Chapter 2. Variables with a negative effect are indicated with a "-" sign.

Although the residual effects of all significant family factors were small when compared in the multiple regression, three variables consistently emerged as important in almost all countries and provinces: parental socio-economic status, the number of books in the home, and family educational support. For all three domains, socio-economic status had small effects on student performance in all countries except Japan. There were small effects of socio-economic status on student performance in all provinces except in Saskatchewan, for all three domains, and in Manitoba, for science performance.

The number of books in the home emerged as an important factor in most countries and in all provinces. The only exceptions were Australia, Finland, Prince Edward Island and Newfoundland in mathematics and Australia in reading. This indicates that the number of books in the home has an influence on student performance that is independent of family socio-economic status and family possessions.

The third consistently important variable is family educational support. After the effects of other variables were taken into account, there was still a small negative relationship between student achievement and educational support received from family members. As was mentioned earlier in the chapter, this finding reflects that students with academic problems are the most likely to receive assistance. In all three domains, only in Japan does this variable not have a relationship with student achievement.

Student cultural activities and parental academic interest also emerged as important factors in Canada. For reading, students who participated in cultural activities outperformed other students in all provinces. This was also an important factor in science achievement in all provinces except New Brunswick and Manitoba. However, it was related to mathematics achievement only in Newfoundland, Prince Edward Island, Quebec and Ontario. Similarly, parental academic interest was an important factor in reading achievement in all provinces except Newfoundland and Quebec; in mathematics achievement in all provinces except Newfoundland, Prince Edward Island, New Brunswick and Quebec; and in science achievement in all provinces except Manitoba.

In Quebec, Manitoba and British Columbia foreign-born students who did not speak French or English at home tended to have lower performance in reading after other factors were taken into account. In Quebec and British Columbia, language spoken at home also showed a negative relationship to science achievement. Internationally, the only other countries where foreign-born students who did not speak a national language or dialect had lower performance in reading, after controlling for other family characteristics, were Germany, Sweden and Switzerland in all three domains and Finland in science.

# Conclusion

While family socio-economic status is an important factor in student achievement, analysis of PISA results revealed many other important family factors. Considered individually, indicators of family background, home environment, parental involvement and parental expectations all exhibited effects on student performance in many countries and provinces. The positive effects of cultural activities and possessions, and parental academic and social interest tended, however, to be more pronounced for reading achievement than for mathematics achievement.

When all of the family characteristics examined were considered together in a multiple regression analysis, parental socio-economic status, the number of books in the home and family educational support emerged as important factors related to student achievement in reading, science and mathematics in virtually all countries and provinces. Participation in cultural activities, and parental academic interest also continued to be strongly related to student performance in reading and science, particularly among Canadian provinces.

Findings indicate that family socio-economic status does not stand alone as the predominant factor influencing student performance. Evidence suggests that parents who are interested in and involved with their children's education and who provide a home environment that stimulates learning can positively influence their children's outcomes.

# Notes

1. See text box describing absolute and relative effects in Chapter 2.
2. Each line segment covers the range of socio-economic status within a country. Finland is included due to its high student performance in reading.
3. Japan is the only country where this pattern is reversed (with positive effects of family educational support on achievement).

# Chapter 4

# The Impact of School Characteristics on Achievement

This chapter explores the influence of certain school characteristics on student performance in the PISA reading assessment. It begins by describing how the student population is distributed between public and private schools, and between schools serving students from families with varying socio-economic statuses (SES). It then examines such school characteristics as disciplinary climate, teacher-student interactions and the adequacy of human and material resources. The chapter explores the following questions about key school factors that influence student academic performance:

- Are there differences in the characteristics of the schools attended by 15-year-olds in the 10 Canadian provinces and in the countries included in this study? What is the extent of these differences?

- Is there a relationship between school characteristics in each jurisdiction and the academic performance of students?

- Which school characteristics are important predictors of academic performance?

The first objective of the analysis is to understand school conditions in each province within an international context. The second objective is to explore the relationship between school factors and student performance on the PISA reading assessment. The chapter concludes with an examination of school characteristics within a multifaceted framework that accounts for interrelationships among the variables. This analysis of the relative effects of these variables allows us to discern which variables have the strongest relationship with achievement.[1]

## School characteristics and student academic performance

This section describes in detail the extent to which schools in Canadian provinces and selected countries differ from each other with respect to a number of characteristics. It also looks at the relationship between these characteristics and student performance. Since the relationship between school characteristics and performance is quite similar in the three domains (reading, mathematics and science), for the sake of simplicity only the results for reading are reported here.

PISA collected information on various aspects of school characteristics from students and principals. This information can be broadly grouped into the following categories: public and private schools, composition of the school population, school climate, teacher-student interactions and adequacy of school resources.

## Public and private schools

The potential academic performance of students in private schools and the impact of private schools on the education system are issues that have recently received increased attention in Canada as well as in other countries. PISA provides information on whether schools were 1) public; 2) private but in receipt of government funding; or 3) private and not in receipt of government funding. For simplicity, the last two groups were combined.

In Canada, close to 94% of 15-year-olds were enrolled in public schools. This figure varies from 84% in Quebec to virtually 100% in Newfoundland, Prince Edward Island, Nova Scotia, and New Brunswick. Internationally, the figure varies from a low of 25% in Belgium to a high of 100% in the Russian Federation (Table 4.1). It should be noted, however, that the nature of private schools in Canada may differ from that of many other countries. Private systems include religious and alternative schools, as well as "elite" schools, and the prevalence of each type of private school varies by province.

In general, in almost all countries and provinces, students attending public schools did not perform as well as students attending private schools. The effect size of the performance disadvantage of public school students was moderate at the Canada level. Within provinces, the negative effect of public school attendance was large in Quebec, Ontario and Manitoba, moderate in Saskatchewan and small in British Columbia. In contrast, the moderate positive effects in Alberta indicate that students attending public schools in Alberta had higher reading scores, on average, than their counterparts attending private schools did. Internationally, the performance disadvantage of public school students was quite large in the United Kingdom, Germany, Belgium and Mexico.

The differences noted above, however, do not warrant conclusions about the relative effectiveness of private schools and public schools. Home circumstances also play an important role in shaping the schooling outcomes of children. Generally, private schools are more accessible to children of higher-income families and, as was evident in Chapter 3 and in the next section, the socio-economic background of the student population has a significant influence on reading test scores.

## Composition of school population

In addition to interacting with teachers and other school personnel, students also interact with their peers while at school. Such interaction forms an important part of the schooling experiences of individual students. Both theory and empirical evidence suggest that children's knowledge and behaviour, including academic outcomes, are influenced by the characteristics or actions of their peers.

Two indicators of the composition of the student population were examined: the school average of an index representing the *socio-economic status (SES)* of parents and the school average of an index representing *family possessions*. The first index was constructed using information on parental occupations. The PISA average of this index is 50. The second index was based on whether students or their families have such items as a dishwasher, a room of their own and educational software. The PISA average of this index is 0, so that negative values indicate lower-than-average scores, and positive values indicate higher-than-average scores.

The school averages of parental SES in the 10 provinces were about the same or higher than the PISA average (Table 4.1). For family possessions, the average index score for all provinces, except Newfoundland, was above the PISA average. Internationally, the school average of parental SES in most of the 14 countries selected for this analysis was close to the PISA average of 50, with the exception of Mexico, which was much lower. Most countries were also similar in terms of the school average of family possessions. The school average of family possessions in the Russian Federation and Mexico, however, was considerably below that of the other countries.

The average socio-economic status of the families of students within schools exerts an influence on the academic performance of individual students. Students from schools where the average family SES was lower, tended not to perform as well as students from schools where the average family SES was higher. The same was generally true for students from schools where the average index of family possessions was lower. The overall effect size of school SES on the reading performance of students was small in all provinces except Ontario, where it was moderate (Table 4.1).

Internationally, the effects are greater, particularly in Germany, Belgium and Mexico, where large effects were found. Only three countries—Finland, Sweden and Japan—showed lower effects of school average SES than Canada.

The effects of the school average of family possessions on reading performance among Canadian provinces exhibited a similar pattern, although the effects were smaller than those for average school SES in every jurisdiction except Manitoba and Saskatchewan. Small effects were found in all countries except France, Germany, Italy, the United States, and Mexico, where effects were moderate. This suggests that, for many countries and provinces, average school SES might be a stronger predictor of academic performance than the school average of family possessions.

## School climate

An orderly and safe environment is a prerequisite for conducting instructional and learning activities in schools. In such environments, both teachers and students are better able to concentrate on learning activities. PISA collected information from both students and principals on their perceptions of school climate.

Students reported on the frequency with which the following occurred in their language arts classes: "students cannot work well," "there is noise and disorder," and "at the start of class, more than five minutes are spent doing nothing." Principals provided information on the extent to which the learning of 15-year-olds was hindered by student absenteeism, class disruption by students, students skipping classes, students showing a lack of respect for teachers, student use of alcohol and drugs, and students intimidating or bullying other students. It should be noted that these variables measure perceptions and may be subject to jurisdictional differences (both cultural and institutional) in how different behaviours are both perceived and tolerated.

These responses were used to construct two separate indices: *disciplinary climate,* representing the average disciplinary climate within the classroom as perceived by students, and *student behaviour,* representing the student behavioural problems within the school as perceived by principals. Both indices were constructed in such a way that the average values for all the countries participating in PISA were zero, with positive or greater values indicating more disciplinary problems, and negative or smaller values indicating fewer such problems.

The Canada-wide average score of 0.14 for the disciplinary climate index was above the overall PISA average of zero, suggesting that, on average, 15-year-old students in Canada were more likely to report disruptions in language arts classrooms than PISA participants overall (Table 4.2). Among provinces, students from Quebec reported the least problematic disciplinary climate while students from Nova Scotia, New Brunswick and Manitoba reported the most. Internationally, students in Japan, the Russian Federation and Switzerland perceived the least problematic disciplinary climates and those in Italy, Sweden and Finland perceived the most.

All provinces also had positive values on the index of principals' perceptions of student behaviour in schools, indicating that student behaviour problems are also perceived to be more serious in Canada than in many other countries. A closer inspection shows that among Canadian provinces, principals reported more student behaviour problems in Prince Edward Island, Nova Scotia, and New Brunswick than in the rest of the country. Principals in the Russian Federation and Finland reported the most problems while those in Japan and Belgium reported the least.

Students who attended schools with either more perceived classroom disciplinary issues or more apparent student behaviour problems had a greater reading performance disadvantage than did those who attended schools with a better climate for learning in most countries and in many provinces (Table 4.2). Small negative effects of classroom disciplinary climate occurred in Prince Edward Island, Nova Scotia, Manitoba, Saskatchewan, Alberta and British Columbia. Internationally, small effects were observed in nine countries. In Japan, effects were moderate.

In general, students from schools with fewer student behaviour problems reported by the principal also tended to have better performance, both within Canada and internationally. Among provinces, small negative effects were found in Ontario, Manitoba, Saskatchewan and Alberta. In all other provinces effects were trivial, with the exception of New Brunswick where a small positive effect of principal reports of student behaviour problems on student performance was observed. Moderate effects occurred in Italy, Japan, the United Kingdom and Belgium. In all other countries effects were small or trivial.

# Teacher-student interactions

Teachers influence student learning through classroom instruction as well as through other channels. It is important for students to have teachers who can motivate and encourage them in their academic pursuits, who treat them fairly, and who are cognisant of their learning needs and can address them effectively. Hence, interactions with teachers form an important part of a student's experience in school. Three indicators of teacher-student interactions are the focus of attention here:

- *Negative teacher behaviour.* This index was constructed based on principals' evaluations of the extent to which student learning is hindered by low expectations of student performance from teachers, poor teacher-student relations, teachers not meeting individual student needs, teacher absenteeism, staff resisting change, teachers being too strict with students, and students not being encouraged to achieve their full potential. Higher positive values indicate more serious perceived negative behaviour on the part of teachers.

- *Teacher support.* This index was constructed based on student evaluations of teacher support. Students were asked questions about the frequency with which the following occurred in language arts classes: interest is shown in every student's learning; students are given an opportunity to express opinions; students are helped with their work; and teachers continue to teach until students understand. Higher positive values mean higher levels of teacher support experienced by students.

- *Teacher-student relations.* This index was constructed based on student evaluations of teacher-student interactions. Students were asked whether they agreed with the following statements: students get along well with most teachers; most teachers are interested in student well-being; most teachers listen to what students have to say; students receive extra help if they need it from teachers; and most teachers treat students fairly. Higher positive values represent more positive relations.

Table 4.3 presents the average scores for each of the 10 Canadian provinces and the selected countries on these three indices and shows the relationship between reading performance and the teacher-student interaction variables. As the international average for all PISA countries on these indices is zero, the average score of *negative teacher behaviour* for Canada as a whole, at -0.12, suggests that, according to principals, negative teacher behaviours were a less significant issue in

Canada. Again, there were differences among provinces. While principals in most of the provinces reported that negative behaviour of teachers was less problematic than did principals in PISA overall, principals in Prince Edward Island, New Brunswick, Quebec, and, to a smaller extent, Manitoba reported more problematic impacts. Internationally, the negative behaviour of teachers was not considered a serious issue in Italy, Japan, Belgium, and Switzerland but was considered to be so in the Russian Federation and Mexico.

Students in Canada overwhelmingly reported a supportive and caring environment in their schools, especially with respect to interactions with teachers. The mean score for Canada was 0.31 for the index of *teacher support* and 0.25 for that of *teacher-student relations*, much higher than the average of all the PISA countries, which was zero. Only students in the United Kingdom, the United States and Australia reported more teacher support, and only students in the United Kingdom, Switzerland, and Mexico reported the same or better teacher-student relations than students in Canada. There was some variation among the provinces, but the variation was relatively small. Such results suggest that, in the eyes of students, teachers in Canada generally do a good job of meeting their needs.

In four countries, students from schools where principals reported a lower impact of negative teacher behaviour tended to have higher performance in reading than did students from schools with more perceived negative teacher behaviour. In these countries, small effects of negative teacher behaviour occurred. Similarly, there were only five countries where there were small to moderate effects of higher levels of teacher support on reading scores. Within Canada, the relationship was trivial between either of these variables and reading performance in every province.

In Japan, the United Kingdom, the United States and Australia there were small to moderate positive effects of teacher-student relations on reading performance (Table 4.3). That is, in these countries, schools where students reported less positive relations with their teachers tended to have lower reading scores. While there was no relationship at the Canada level, small effects of teacher-student relations on reading performance occurred in Newfoundland and Saskatchewan.

# School resources

This section examines two aspects of school resources: human and material. Two variables were used to represent human resources. The first is the extent of teacher shortage in a school, and the second is the level of teacher commitment and morale in a school as rated by principals. There were also two variables representing the adequacy of a school's physical resources. More specifically, the four variables are:

- *Teacher shortage.* This index was created using principals' responses to questions on the extent to which the learning of 15-year-olds was hindered by the shortage or inadequacy of: teachers, teachers of test language or literature, teachers of mathematics, and teachers of science. Higher positive values indicate a more serious shortage of teachers.

- *Teacher morale and commitment.* The creation of this index was based on responses about the extent to which the following statements were true: the morale of teachers in this school is high; teachers work with enthusiasm; teachers take pride in this school; and teachers value academic achievement. Higher positive values indicate higher teacher morale and commitment.

- *Inadequacy of instructional resources.* This index reflects the extent to which the learning of 15-year-olds in the study was hindered by inadequacy in the following types of resources: instructional material (e.g., textbooks); computers for instruction; library materials; multimedia resources for instruction; science laboratory equipment; and facilities for the fine arts. Higher positive values indicate a greater inadequacy of resources.

- *Inadequacy of material resources.* This index represents the extent to which the following were detrimental to the learning of 15-year-olds in a school: poor condition of buildings; poor condition of heating, cooling and/or lighting systems; and lack of instructional space. Higher positive values indicate a greater inadequacy of material resources.

As Table 4.4 shows, Canada scores 0.01 on the teacher shortage index, and 0.08 on the index of teacher morale and commitment. The international average for all PISA countries on these indices is zero. These figures indicate that, compared with all PISA countries on average, Canadian principals reported typical levels of impact of teacher shortage and teacher morale and commitment. However, these average figures mask two facts. First, the problem of teacher shortage seems more serious in 7 out of 10 provinces than in other PISA countries, on average. Second, there were vast differences among provinces with respect to the seriousness of the problem.

While principals in British Columbia, Quebec and Ontario did not consider teacher shortage to be a problem, it was considered a serious problem by principals in Newfoundland, Prince Edward Island, Nova Scotia, and New Brunswick and, to a lesser extent, in Manitoba, Saskatchewan, and Alberta. In fact, principals in Newfoundland, Prince Edward Island, Nova Scotia, and New Brunswick were more likely to report an adverse effect of teacher shortage on the learning of 15-year-olds than were principals in most of the other 13 countries, with responses comparable to the Russian Federation and Mexico. However, principals in Canada also gave high ratings to the morale and commitment of teachers in their schools, especially those in Prince Edward Island, Saskatchewan, Alberta and British Columbia.

Table 4.4 shows that in many countries students attending schools in which teacher shortage was less of a problem generally had higher reading scores. Small negative effects of reported teacher shortage on reading performance occurred in six of the fourteen countries. Similarly, small positive effects of teacher morale on reading performance were found in seven countries indicating that schools with higher levels of teacher morale and commitment tended to have higher reading scores. Among provinces there was little to no relationship between reports of teacher shortage or teacher morale and student performance.

According to principals, instructional and material resources were less of a constraint to student learning in Canada as a whole than in the PISA countries, on average, as is shown by the score of -0.24 and -0.35 on the two indices in Table 4.4. In fact, this was true for half of the countries studied here. With respect to the inadequacy of instructional resources, the exceptions in Canada were Newfoundland, Nova Scotia and Manitoba, where principals felt that the lack of instructional resources was detrimental to the learning of 15-year-olds in their schools. Internationally, the problem was particularly acute in the Russian Federation, Mexico and the United Kingdom. In terms of school material resources, only principals in Nova Scotia reported a problem more serious than the PISA average. Internationally, principals in the Russian Federation, the United Kingdom and Mexico were the most likely to have considered constrained resources to be a serious issue in their schools.

Do students from schools with more resources outperform those with fewer resources? In eight countries, the answer was yes. However, the effect of instructional resource adequacy was trivial in Canada and in the provinces. In fact, the moderate effect occurring in Mexico was more than 5 times greater than that of Canada.

There is little evidence of a relationship between the inadequacy of material resources and student performance in most jurisdictions. In all provinces, there were no conclusive relationships between principals' reports of material resource adequacy and student performance. Internationally, small effects of reports of material resource inadequacy on student performance occurred only in the Russian Federation, Belgium and Mexico.

# The relative importance of school factors in explaining reading performance

The previous section described the conditions of Canadian schools in an international context. It also demonstrated that a few school characteristics can be used to differentiate high-performing from low-performing students. Are some factors more important than others in predicting student performance in each of the jurisdictions? Are there differences between the jurisdictions in the importance of various factors in predicting student performance once the relationships between these variables are taken into account?

In order to answer these questions, multiple regression analyses were conducted for each jurisdiction, using the variables representing school characteristics listed above. Standardised coefficients were obtained to indicate the relative effect of each of the variables on student reading performance in each jurisdiction.

Table 4.5 presents results of this multiple regression analysis. It shows the magnitude of the relative impact of the variables as small (s), medium (m), or large (l), using the criteria outlined in Chapter 2. Variables with a negative effect are indicated with a "-" sign.

Either or both of the composition characteristics of the school population—the school averages of parental socio-economic status and family possessions—were important predictors of reading performance in all countries, except Finland, and in all provinces, except New Brunswick. This indicates that students from schools attended by students from predominantly high-SES backgrounds or well-to-do families had higher reading scores, even after taking into consideration public

or private funding, disciplinary climate, teacher-student interaction and school resources.

For Canada as a whole, only average family socio-economic status within schools and average family possessions within schools appeared as important variables when other school factors were taken into account. Within provinces, however, several other school characteristics also had an important influence on student performance.

Student perceptions of disciplinary climate problems in the classroom and principal perceptions of student behaviour problems were also related to student outcomes in several jurisdictions, after other school characteristics were taken into account. Disciplinary climate emerged as an important factor in five countries, Italy, Japan, Australia, the Russian Federation and Mexico and in four provinces, Nova Scotia, Quebec, Manitoba and Alberta. Student behaviour problems were also linked to student performance in Italy, Japan, the United Kingdom, Belgium and Switzerland. In New Brunswick reports of behaviour problems were positively linked to student performance, indicating that students performed better in schools where principals perceived more problematic behaviour.

The performance disadvantage observed in public schools largely disappeared after other school factors were taken into consideration. In fact, the only significant effects of public school attendance in Canada were positive in Alberta and Ontario. In other words, after taking the effect of other school characteristics into consideration, including school average parental SES, public school attendance was associated with higher individual performance. This relationship was consistent with that observed in Switzerland and Mexico. In Belgium, however, the effect of public school attendance remained negative.

When considered in combination with other school characteristics, variables representing teacher-student interactions and school resources were also related to reading performance in a few jurisdictions. In six countries and one province, one or more of the teacher-student interaction variables or the school resources variables was a significant predictor of variation in reading test scores. For variables representing teacher-student interactions, students from schools where students experienced better relations with teachers and schools where students reported less teacher support (possibly where fewer students have learning difficulties) tended to perform better in a few jurisdictions. With respect to adequacy of instructional resources, only France and Italy had significant effects. In Germany, reports of teacher shortages had a negative relationship with student achievement. In Italy, however, students in schools where principals perceived greater problems with teacher shortage also tended to have higher performance.

It is important to note that one cannot conclude that schools with the characteristics mentioned above are necessarily effective at *improving* student learning. In order to find out what types of schools are more or less effective at improving student learning, it is necessary to have information at two or more points in time. Since the PISA data were collected at only one point in time, it is impossible to know how much a student has *gained* in learning or what are the cumulative effects of the characteristics of schools on achievement. Furthermore, the findings summarised above refer to entire student populations, masking considerable variation within each jurisdiction and within each school. In addition, individual students from specific subpopulations, such as those from disadvantaged backgrounds, those from language minorities, and those with special learning needs, may have either lower or higher average performances in schools with the above-mentioned characteristics. More detailed analysis of the academic performance of specific populations is needed.

# Conclusion

Schools play an important role in students' acquisition of knowledge and skills, as well as in the general development of children and youth. Individuals enter school with different abilities, learning skills, attitudes and aspirations. The school experiences children go through can reduce such initial differences between them so that they can reach the end of their schooling with comparable levels of academic achievement. However, school experiences can also amplify the differences so that students end up with quite different schooling outcomes. With the importance of school characteristics in mind, this analysis explored differences in school characteristics among countries and provinces and the relationship between school characteristics and reading achievement.

As many variables included in the analysis of school characteristics were based on student and principal perceptions, international comparisons should be interpreted with the understanding that school infrastructures, cultural sensitivities, and tolerance levels differ among the jurisdictions. As a result, variables representing principal and student perceptions of school characteristics are not objective measures of these characteristics.

It is also important to note that the PISA assessment captured the characteristics of students' current schools. A student's performance in reading, as measured in PISA, however, is not only influenced by the characteristics of their current school, but also by the characteristics of schools that they have attended in the past. Thus, the impact of school characteristics on student performance would likely be greater if cumulative effects of school characteristics could be measured and if more objective measures of school characteristics could be made.

Nonetheless, when considered individually, many of the school variables examined had a relationship with the performance of students in reading across countries and provinces. Among provinces, school average socio-economic status, school average of family possessions, and to a lesser extent student reports of more positive classroom disciplinary climate, student reports of more positive teacher-student relations, and principal reports of fewer student behaviour problems had a positive relationship with reading performance.

When all of the school characteristics examined were considered together in a multiple regression analysis, the data showed that, both in many Canadian provinces and in other countries, students from schools with the following characteristics tended to have higher student performance: schools with students from higher socio-economic family backgrounds and/or more well-to-do families; and schools with reports of a positive disciplinary climate and with fewer reported problems with student behaviour.

# Note

1.  See text box describing absolute and relative effects in Chapter 2.

# Conclusion

Ensuring that Canadian youth are equipped with the skills and knowledge they need to compete in the knowledge-based economy is an objective shared by all levels of government in Canada. The OECD Programme for International Student Assessment (PISA) provides the opportunity to measure the proficiency of Canadian youth at age 15 in reading, mathematics and science within an international context.

Both the labour market and society in general place a high premium on reading skills, since these are vital tools for effectively receiving, understanding and communicating information. In 2000, the major focus of the PISA assessment was reading literacy, with mathematical and scientific literacy as minor domains.

The PISA 2000 assessment was administered to more than 250,000 students in 32 countries. In Canada, the assessment was administered to approximately 30,000 students. This report compares the achievement of Canadian youth with that of youth from thirteen other countries. These countries were selected for comparison with Canada and the provinces because of their similarities to Canada, their record of high achievement or their relevance to Canada. They include the other G8 countries (France, Germany, Italy, Japan, United Kingdom, United States and Russia), as well as Australia, Belgium, Finland, Mexico, Sweden and Switzerland.

PISA results indicate that Canadian students performed well compared with other countries, ranking second in reading, sixth in mathematics and fifth in science. Canada is among a select few countries that scored near the top in all three domains. Only Finland performed significantly better than Canada in reading,

only Korea and Japan performed significantly better in mathematics and only Korea, Japan and Finland performed significantly better in science.

While this was the first time that the PISA tests were administered, this is not the first program to test international achievement. Although previous international studies are not directly comparable because of differences in frameworks, age differences and differences in some participating countries, it is fair to say that Canada's achievement ranking relative to other countries has been improving over time. Canada has risen from a mid-ranked country to one of the top-ranked countries. This does not tell us *how much* achievement has actually improved, however, or indeed if it has improved at all. It simply indicates that Canada has advanced in relation to other countries.

Despite the overall high achievement of Canadian young people, there are reasons to be concerned about the differences in achievement scores that exist between and within provinces. Differences in average scores and in the proportions of top students are large enough to imply social and economic consequences for some. Although at or above the middle of the international range, the average scores of students in Newfoundland, Prince Edward Island, Nova Scotia and New Brunswick were significantly below the Canadian average in reading, mathematics and science. The performance of students in Alberta was significantly above the Canadian average in all three domains, as was the performance of Quebec students in mathematics and science.

Using the cross-country PISA results, the OECD defined five levels of reading proficiency. As expected, provinces and countries with the highest overall scores also had the highest proportion of students at level 5 and the lowest proportion at or below level 1. Approximately 17% of Canadian youth were at level 5, and less than 10% were at or below level 1. Again, the figures vary widely within Canada. While New Brunswick had more students at or below level 1 than other provinces, Alberta had more students at level 5. In fact, compared with all participating countries, Alberta had the highest proportion of students at level 5.

Canada's high scores were not gained at the cost of higher inequality in results. In all participating countries, students from high socio-economic backgrounds performed better than students from low socio-economic backgrounds. Canada, along with Japan and Finland, exhibited far less variation in scores between students in these two socio-economic groups than did most other countries. This suggests that achievement scores are more equivalent among students with different socio-economic backgrounds in Canada, than they are in many other countries.

While Canada is noted for its equitable achievement results, our national performance masks significant variation across the provinces. For example, students from Saskatchewan exhibited less variation in reading achievement by family socio-economic background than did students in other provinces. Performance of students with a mid-to-high socio-economic background in these provinces, however, fell below that of several other provinces. Alberta and Quebec, on the other hand, had generally the highest achievement scores across all levels of family socio-economic background, yet had greater variation in scores across socio-economic groups. Among the provinces, Newfoundland had the greatest variation across socio-economic groups in reading and science performance and Nova Scotia in mathematics performance.

A route to improving the average reading ability of youth in all of the provinces lies in improving reading skills among economically or socially disadvantaged youth. Monitoring the performance of students within these economic groups in future PISA cycles will be an important means of evaluating Canada's success in meeting this challenge.

Particular attention may also be focussed on students enrolled in francophone minority school systems. Among the four provinces where data were collected for francophone minority school systems

separately, Nova Scotia, New Brunswick, Ontario and Manitoba, students in these systems performed at a significantly lower level in reading and science than did students enrolled in anglophone majority systems. In Quebec, on the other hand, students enrolled in the anglophone school system performed as well as those enrolled in the francophone school system.

These results will need to be contextualised. For example, further analysis will clarify the extent to which important background variables, such as the main language spoken at home, contribute to these differences.

Girls performed significantly better than boys on the reading test in all countries and in all Canadian provinces. In contrast, there were few significant differences between girls and boys in mathematics and science. The lower average result for boys is a source of concern, since poor reading performance can have a profound effect on performance in other subjects.

Canadian boys have higher high school dropout rates than do girls and are less likely than girls to be studying at the undergraduate level in university.[1] This, added to PISA results, may indicate that boys are at greater risk of not having the reading skills required for successful integration into the labour market in the future.

Differences in reading performance between girls and boys were, however, strongly linked to differences between the genders in key individual characteristics measured in PISA, particularly reading behaviours including enjoyment of reading. When the effects of these characteristics are taken into consideration, gender no longer appears to have a significant effect on reading performance. There was, however, a small effect favouring boys in mathematics and science in most countries and provinces, when other characteristics were taken into consideration.

This counter intuitive result occurred because the contextual information collected in PISA 2000 was able to explain variation in reading achievement between girls and boys. Gender differences in mathematics and science will be more comprehensively examined following future cycles of PISA when these domains will hold the major focus.

Among the individual characteristics of students examined, enjoyment of reading and students' career expectations were consistently positively related to reading proficiency across countries and provinces.

Using data from the Canadian Youth in Transition Survey (YITS), a preliminary analysis was undertaken to better understand how working while studying mediates achievement. In all provinces, students without jobs during the school year had significantly higher average reading performance than did working students. Most provinces did not, however, have significant differences favouring non-working students in mathematics or science achievement. Nonetheless, in all three domains, as the hours worked per week increased, performance tended to decline.

Previous studies have shown, however, that working a limited number of hours while in school does not increase the probability of dropping out of high school. The longer-term impact of combining work and study at age 15 on education and labour-market outcomes will be clarified through future research that takes advantage of the longitudinal nature of YITS. For example, students working a limited number of hours while in school might have lower achievement results, but might engage in valuable workplace experiences or might develop useful skills and knowledge. What is critical for these students is that their work experiences do not jeopardize their completion of secondary education.

Among family characteristics, the socio-economic background of the family and the number of books in the home were factors influencing reading achievement. Other positive influences were attendance at concerts, museums and other cultural events and parents who discussed political or social issues, books or television shows with their children.

Findings indicate that family socio-economic status does not stand alone as the predominant factor influencing student achievement. Evidence suggests that parents who are interested in and involved with their children's education and who provide a home environment that stimulates learning can positively influence their children's academic outcomes. All Canadian parents need to be aware of the positive influence they can have on the academic achievement of their children.

In Canada, education is essential for building valuable human capital and providing equal opportunities for all youth. The examination of school factors identified some – both positive and negative – that can be addressed by schools to enhance student achievement. Among provinces, principals' reports of positive teacher-student relations, principals' reports of better student behaviour, students' reports of more positive teacher-student relations, and students' reports of more positive classroom disciplinary climates had a positive relationship with student proficiency in reading.

Not only is the socio-economic status of students' families related to their achievement, but a concentration of students with either high or low socio-economic backgrounds in a school also influences achievement of students. Students who attended schools with a low-average family socio-economic status (SES) tended to perform at a lower level than those from high-average SES schools. Even though the effect of average school SES on reading performance for Canada was one of the smallest among the countries examined in this report, it is significant. Since a key objective of Canadian schools is to achieve equity among schools educating children with different socio-economic backgrounds, these results require further assessment and consideration.

This report has both identified sub-populations with lower performance and characteristics of students, families and schools that are related to lower student performance. The PISA 2000 study provides more detailed information that will be explored to better understand the characteristics of lower-performing students and the circumstances that may have contributed to their outcomes on the PISA assessment. In the longer-term, the Youth in Transition Survey will continue to follow the progress of these students to enhance our understanding of how achievement at age 15, as well as current personal, family and school characteristics, contribute to successful educational and labour-market transitions in the future.

Overall, what is striking about these Canadian results is that despite having many different jurisdictions that deliver education, the outcomes of the PISA assessment are quite similar for the majority of provinces. As well, this Pan-Canadian report shows that no single factor, by itself, can explain differences in reading achievement. School, student and family characteristics work alone and in combination to influence the success of students. Nevertheless, the performance of Canadian youth in the PISA assessment appears promising for their future, and for the future of Canada.

# Note

1. Human Resources Development Canada and Statistics Canada (1998), *High School May Not Be Enough,* Human Resources Development Canada catalogue no. SP-105-05-98E and Statistics Canada catalogue no. 81-585-XBE, Ottawa.

# ANNEX A: TABLES

The enclosed tables are based on the Organization for Economic Cooperation and Development Programme for International Student Assessment, 2000, unless otherwise noted.

The *standard error* associated with the estimates presented is included in parenthesis. The *confidence interval*, when presented, represents the range within which the score for the population is likely to fall, with 95% probability.

Several tables in this publication present average scores along with their standard errors. In order to estimate whether two averages are statistically significantly different, the following formula can be applied to approximate a 95% confidence interval.

Approximate Confidence Interval = Average score ± 2 x Standard Error

This approximate confidence interval gives a range within which the true average is likely to fall. If two confidence intervals do not overlap, then there is a significant statistical difference between the two averages. It should be noted that this formula is approximate because it estimates a confidence interval that is slightly higher than the 95% level of confidence. As a result, there is a small risk that a significant difference will be identified as insignificant.

## Standardised effects

*Standardized effects* result from regression analysis performed to examine the extent a variable(s) influence(s) achievement. For some of the analysis in this report, the impact of various factors on student achievement has been measured using *standardized effects*. In some cases similar analysis was presented in the international OECD report using an unstandardized measure. Standardized effects were chosen for the presentation of the data in this report because they allow for a fuller picture of how various outcomes are related to predictors within each country by taking into account the variability of student performance. For example, reading enjoyment may increase performance by 40 points in two separate countries; in one country, this may not significantly change a student's performance relative to his or her peers, but in a country such as Canada—where there is less variability in scores—it may move a student from the lowest quartile into the highest quartile. Thus, for Canadian analysis, standardized effects provide a better tool for understanding the factors that influence achievement of Canadian students.

The following thresholds in the absolute values of the effect size statistic were used to judge the magnitude of the differences:

Trivial:      Less than |0.10|

Small:        Between |0.10| and |0.30|

Moderate:     Between |0.30| and |0.50|

Large:        Greater than |0.50|


Symbols and abbreviations

. .   missing data

N/A   not applicable

S     estimates suppressed due to small sample sizes.

## TABLE 1.1

### Averages and Confidence Intervals: READING

| Country and province | Average | Standard error | Confidence interval (+ -) |
|---|---|---|---|
| Alberta | 550 | (3.3) | 6.5 |
| Finland | 546 | (2.6) | 5.1 |
| British Columbia | 538 | (2.9) | 5.7 |
| Quebec | 536 | (3.0) | 6.0 |
| **CANADA** | **534** | **(1.6)** | **3.1** |
| Ontario | 533 | (3.3) | 6.5 |
| Manitoba | 529 | (3.5) | 7.0 |
| Saskatchewan | 529 | (2.7) | 5.3 |
| New Zealand | 529 | (2.8) | 5.5 |
| Australia | 528 | (3.5) | 7.0 |
| Ireland | 527 | (3.2) | 6.4 |
| Korea | 525 | (2.4) | 4.8 |
| United Kingdom | 523 | (2.6) | 5.1 |
| Japan | 522 | (5.2) | 10.4 |
| Nova Scotia | 521 | (2.3) | 4.5 |
| Prince Edward Island | 517 | (2.4) | 4.8 |
| Newfoundland | 517 | (2.8) | 5.6 |
| Sweden | 516 | (2.2) | 4.4 |
| Austria | 507 | (2.4) | 4.8 |
| Belgium | 507 | (3.6) | 7.1 |
| Iceland | 507 | (1.5) | 2.9 |
| Norway | 505 | (2.8) | 5.6 |
| France | 505 | (2.7) | 5.4 |
| United States | 504 | (7.0) | 14.0 |
| New Brunswick | 501 | (1.8) | 3.5 |
| Denmark | 497 | (2.4) | 4.7 |
| Switzerland | 494 | (4.2) | 8.4 |
| Spain | 493 | (2.7) | 5.4 |
| Czech Republic | 492 | (2.4) | 4.7 |
| Italy | 487 | (2.9) | 5.8 |
| Germany | 484 | (2.5) | 4.9 |
| Liechtenstein | 483 | (4.1) | 8.2 |
| Hungary | 480 | (4.0) | 7.9 |
| Poland | 479 | (4.5) | 8.9 |
| Greece | 474 | (5.0) | 9.9 |
| Portugal | 470 | (4.5) | 9.0 |
| Russian Federation | 462 | (4.2) | 8.3 |
| Latvia | 458 | (5.3) | 10.3 |
| Luxembourg | 441 | (1.6) | 3.2 |
| Mexico | 422 | (3.3) | 6.6 |
| Brazil | 396 | (3.1) | 6.2 |

## TABLE 1.2

### Averages and Confidence Intervals: MATHEMATICS

| Country and province | Average | Standard error | Confidence interval (+ -) |
|---|---|---|---|
| Japan | 557 | (5.5) | 10.9 |
| Quebec | 550 | (2.7) | 5.4 |
| Alberta | 547 | (3.3) | 6.6 |
| Korea | 547 | (2.8) | 5.5 |
| New Zealand | 537 | (3.1) | 6.3 |
| Finland | 536 | (2.1) | 4.3 |
| British Columbia | 534 | (2.8) | 5.6 |
| Australia | 533 | (3.5) | 6.9 |
| Manitoba | 533 | (3.7) | 7.3 |
| **CANADA** | **533** | **(1.4)** | **2.8** |
| Switzerland | 529 | (4.4) | 8.7 |
| United Kingdom | 529 | (2.5) | 5.0 |
| Saskatchewan | 525 | (2.9) | 5.8 |
| Ontario | 524 | (2.9) | 5.8 |
| Belgium | 520 | (3.9) | 7.8 |
| France | 517 | (2.7) | 5.4 |
| Austria | 515 | (2.5) | 5.0 |
| Denmark | 514 | (2.4) | 4.9 |
| Iceland | 514 | (2.3) | 4.5 |
| Liechtenstein | 514 | (7.0) | 13.9 |
| Nova Scotia | 513 | (2.8) | 5.6 |
| Prince Edward Island | 512 | (3.7) | 7.4 |
| Sweden | 510 | (2.5) | 4.9 |
| Newfoundland | 509 | (3.0) | 5.9 |
| New Brunswick | 506 | (2.2) | 4.4 |
| Ireland | 503 | (2.7) | 5.4 |
| Norway | 499 | (2.8) | 5.5 |
| Czech Republic | 498 | (2.8) | 5.5 |
| United States | 493 | (7.6) | 15.2 |
| Germany | 490 | (2.5) | 5.0 |
| Hungary | 488 | (4.0) | 8.0 |
| Russian Federation | 478 | (5.5) | 10.9 |
| Spain | 476 | (3.1) | 6.2 |
| Poland | 470 | (5.5) | 10.9 |
| Latvia | 463 | (4.5) | 8.7 |
| Italy | 457 | (2.9) | 5.8 |
| Portugal | 454 | (4.1) | 8.1 |
| Greece | 447 | (5.6) | 11.1 |
| Luxembourg | 446 | (2.0) | 4.0 |
| Mexico | 387 | (3.4) | 6.7 |
| Brazil | 334 | (3.7) | 7.4 |

## TABLE 1.3

### Averages and Confidence Intervals: SCIENCE

| Country and province | Average | Standard error | Confidence interval (+ -) |
|---|---|---|---|
| Korea | 552 | (2.7) | 5.4 |
| Japan | 550 | (5.5) | 10.9 |
| Alberta | 546 | (3.5) | 6.9 |
| Quebec | 541 | (3.4) | 6.7 |
| Finland | 538 | (2.5) | 4.9 |
| British Columbia | 533 | (3.2) | 6.4 |
| United Kingdom | 532 | (2.7) | 5.3 |
| **CANADA** | **529** | **(1.6)** | **3.1** |
| New Zealand | 528 | (2.4) | 4.8 |
| Australia | 528 | (3.5) | 6.9 |
| Manitoba | 527 | (3.6) | 7.1 |
| Ontario | 522 | (3.4) | 6.8 |
| Saskatchewan | 522 | (3.0) | 5.9 |
| Austria | 519 | (2.5) | 5.1 |
| Newfoundland | 516 | (3.4) | 6.7 |
| Nova Scotia | 516 | (3.0) | 6.0 |
| Ireland | 513 | (3.2) | 6.3 |
| Sweden | 512 | (2.5) | 5.0 |
| Czech Republic | 511 | (2.4) | 4.8 |
| Prince Edward Island | 508 | (2.7) | 5.4 |
| France | 500 | (3.2) | 6.3 |
| Norway | 500 | (2.7) | 5.5 |
| United States | 499 | (7.3) | 14.6 |
| New Brunswick | 497 | (2.3) | 4.5 |
| Hungary | 496 | (4.2) | 8.3 |
| Iceland | 496 | (2.2) | 4.3 |
| Belgium | 496 | (4.3) | 8.5 |
| Switzerland | 496 | (4.4) | 8.8 |
| Spain | 491 | (3.0) | 5.9 |
| Germany | 487 | (2.4) | 4.8 |
| Poland | 483 | (5.1) | 10.2 |
| Denmark | 481 | (2.8) | 5.6 |
| Italy | 478 | (3.1) | 6.1 |
| Liechtenstein | 476 | (7.1) | 14.1 |
| Greece | 461 | (4.9) | 9.7 |
| Russian Federation | 460 | (4.7) | 9.4 |
| Latvia | 460 | (5.6) | 11.0 |
| Portugal | 459 | (4.0) | 8.0 |
| Luxembourg | 443 | (2.3) | 4.6 |
| Mexico | 422 | (3.2) | 6.3 |
| Brazil | 375 | (3.3) | 6.5 |

## TABLE 1.4

### Averages and Confidence Intervals: READING RETRIEVING

| Country and province | Average | Standard error | Confidence interval (+ -) |
|---|---|---|---|
| Finland | 556 | (2.8) | 5.5 |
| Alberta | 549 | (3.5) | 7.0 |
| Australia | 536 | (3.7) | 7.4 |
| British Columbia | 535 | (3.1) | 6.1 |
| New Zealand | 535 | (2.8) | 5.6 |
| Quebec | 531 | (3.2) | 6.4 |
| **CANADA** | **530** | **(1.7)** | **3.3** |
| Korea | 530 | (2.5) | 4.9 |
| Ontario | 528 | (3.5) | 7.0 |
| Saskatchewan | 527 | (2.7) | 5.4 |
| Manitoba | 527 | (3.6) | 7.2 |
| Japan | 526 | (5.5) | 10.9 |
| Ireland | 524 | (3.3) | 6.5 |
| United Kingdom | 523 | (2.5) | 5.0 |
| Nova Scotia | 516 | (2.7) | 5.3 |
| Sweden | 516 | (2.4) | 4.8 |
| France | 515 | (3.0) | 5.9 |
| Belgium | 515 | (3.9) | 7.8 |
| Newfoundland | 512 | (2.9) | 5.7 |
| Prince Edward Island | 512 | (2.8) | 5.5 |
| Norway | 505 | (2.9) | 5.8 |
| Austria | 502 | (2.3) | 4.6 |
| Iceland | 500 | (1.6) | 3.1 |
| United States | 499 | (7.4) | 14.6 |
| Switzerland | 498 | (4.4) | 8.8 |
| Denmark | 498 | (2.8) | 5.5 |
| New Brunswick | 494 | (1.8) | 3.6 |
| Liechtenstein | 492 | (4.9) | 9.7 |
| Italy | 488 | (3.1) | 6.2 |
| Spain | 483 | (3.0) | 5.9 |
| Germany | 483 | (2.4) | 4.8 |
| Czech Republic | 481 | (2.7) | 5.3 |
| Hungary | 478 | (4.4) | 8.8 |
| Poland | 475 | (5.0) | 9.9 |
| Portugal | 455 | (4.9) | 9.7 |
| Latvia | 451 | (5.7) | 11.2 |
| Russian Federation | 451 | (4.9) | 9.8 |
| Greece | 450 | (5.4) | 10.7 |
| Luxembourg | 433 | (1.6) | 3.2 |
| Mexico | 402 | (3.9) | 7.7 |
| Brazil | 365 | (3.4) | 6.8 |

## TABLE 1.5

### Averages and Confidence Intervals:
### READING INTERPRETING

| Country and province | Average | Standard error | Confidence interval (+ -) |
|---|---|---|---|
| Finland | 555 | (2.9) | 5.7 |
| Alberta | 546 | (3.3) | 6.6 |
| Quebec | 538 | (3.0) | 6.0 |
| British Columbia | 534 | (2.8) | 5.6 |
| **CANADA** | **532** | **(1.6)** | **3.1** |
| Ontario | 529 | (3.3) | 6.5 |
| Australia | 527 | (3.5) | 7.0 |
| Ireland | 526 | (3.3) | 6.5 |
| New Zealand | 526 | (2.7) | 5.4 |
| Manitoba | 526 | (3.3) | 6.6 |
| Saskatchewan | 525 | (2.6) | 5.2 |
| Korea | 525 | (2.3) | 4.6 |
| Sweden | 522 | (2.1) | 4.2 |
| Japan | 518 | (5.0) | 9.9 |
| Nova Scotia | 517 | (2.4) | 4.8 |
| Iceland | 514 | (1.4) | 2.9 |
| United Kingdom | 514 | (2.5) | 5.0 |
| Prince Edward Island | 513 | (2.5) | 4.9 |
| Belgium | 512 | (3.2) | 6.3 |
| Newfoundland | 512 | (2.7) | 5.3 |
| Austria | 508 | (2.4) | 4.9 |
| France | 506 | (2.7) | 5.4 |
| Norway | 505 | (2.8) | 5.5 |
| United States | 505 | (7.1) | 14.1 |
| New Brunswick | 500 | (1.7) | 3.5 |
| Czech Republic | 500 | (2.4) | 4.8 |
| Switzerland | 496 | (4.2) | 8.3 |
| Denmark | 494 | (2.4) | 4.8 |
| Spain | 491 | (2.6) | 5.2 |
| Italy | 489 | (2.6) | 5.2 |
| Germany | 488 | (2.5) | 4.9 |
| Liechtenstein | 484 | (4.5) | 8.9 |
| Poland | 482 | (4.3) | 8.5 |
| Hungary | 480 | (3.8) | 7.5 |
| Greece | 475 | (4.5) | 8.9 |
| Portugal | 473 | (4.3) | 8.5 |
| Russian Federation | 468 | (4.0) | 7.9 |
| Latvia | 459 | (4.9) | 9.5 |
| Luxembourg | 446 | (1.6) | 3.1 |
| Mexico | 419 | (2.9) | 5.8 |
| Brazil | 400 | (3.0) | 6.0 |

## TABLE 1.6

### Averages and Confidence Intervals:
### READING REFLECTING

| Country and province | Average | Standard error | Confidence interval (+ -) |
|---|---|---|---|
| Alberta | 559 | (3.5) | 6.9 |
| British Columbia | 547 | (2.8) | 5.6 |
| Ontario | 544 | (3.2) | 6.4 |
| **CANADA** | **542** | **(1.6)** | **3.1** |
| Saskatchewan | 539 | (2.6) | 5.1 |
| United Kingdom | 539 | (2.5) | 5.0 |
| Manitoba | 539 | (3.3) | 6.6 |
| Quebec | 537 | (3.1) | 6.1 |
| Ireland | 533 | (3.1) | 6.2 |
| Nova Scotia | 533 | (2.4) | 4.8 |
| Finland | 533 | (2.7) | 5.4 |
| Japan | 530 | (5.4) | 10.8 |
| New Zealand | 529 | (2.9) | 5.8 |
| Newfoundland | 529 | (2.6) | 5.2 |
| Prince Edward Island | 528 | (2.5) | 4.9 |
| Australia | 526 | (3.4) | 6.9 |
| Korea | 526 | (2.6) | 5.2 |
| Austria | 512 | (2.7) | 5.4 |
| Sweden | 510 | (2.3) | 4.5 |
| New Brunswick | 510 | (1.9) | 3.8 |
| United States | 507 | (7.1) | 14.1 |
| Norway | 506 | (3.0) | 5.9 |
| Spain | 506 | (2.8) | 5.6 |
| Iceland | 501 | (1.3) | 2.6 |
| Denmark | 500 | (2.6) | 5.2 |
| Belgium | 497 | (4.3) | 8.6 |
| France | 496 | (2.9) | 5.7 |
| Greece | 495 | (5.6) | 11.1 |
| Switzerland | 488 | (4.8) | 9.6 |
| Czech Republic | 485 | (2.6) | 5.2 |
| Italy | 483 | (3.1) | 6.2 |
| Hungary | 481 | (4.3) | 8.5 |
| Portugal | 480 | (4.5) | 9.0 |
| Germany | 478 | (2.9) | 5.7 |
| Poland | 477 | (4.7) | 9.4 |
| Liechtenstein | 468 | (5.7) | 11.4 |
| Latvia | 458 | (5.3) | 10.3 |
| Russian Federation | 455 | (4.0) | 7.9 |
| Mexico | 446 | (3.7) | 7.4 |
| Luxembourg | 442 | (1.9) | 3.7 |
| Brazil | 417 | (3.3) | 6.6 |

## TABLE 1.7

### Reading Scores at 5th, 10th, 25th, 50th, 75th, 90th and 95th Percentiles

| Country and province | 5th percentile | | 10th percentile | | 25th percentile | | 50th percentile | | 75th percentile | | 90th percentile | | 95th percentile | |
|---|---|---|---|---|---|---|---|---|---|---|---|---|---|---|
| **CANADA** | **371** | **(3.8)** | **410** | **(2.5)** | **472** | **(2.0)** | **540** | **(1.7)** | **600** | **(1.5)** | **652** | **(1.9)** | **681** | **(2.8)** |
| France | 344 | (6.3) | 381 | (5.3) | 444 | (4.4) | 511 | (3.1) | 570 | (2.3) | 618 | (2.7) | 645 | (3.6) |
| United States | 320 | (11.2) | 363 | (11.5) | 436 | (8.8) | 511 | (7.0) | 577 | (6.4) | 636 | (5.9) | 669 | (7.0) |
| United Kingdom | 352 | (4.9) | 391 | (3.9) | 458 | (2.9) | 527 | (2.7) | 595 | (3.5) | 651 | (4.0) | 682 | (4.9) |
| Germany | 284 | (7.5) | 335 | (5.7) | 417 | (4.0) | 494 | (3.1) | 562 | (3.1) | 619 | (2.6) | 650 | (3.4) |
| Japan | 366 | (11.7) | 407 | (10.2) | 471 | (7.0) | 530 | (4.9) | 582 | (4.5) | 625 | (4.6) | 650 | (4.5) |
| Italy | 331 | (8.8) | 367 | (5.9) | 429 | (4.1) | 492 | (3.2) | 552 | (3.2) | 601 | (2.6) | 627 | (3.3) |
| Russian Federation | 305 | (7.0) | 340 | (5.8) | 400 | (5.0) | 464 | (4.2) | 526 | (4.3) | 579 | (4.2) | 608 | (5.3) |
| Australia | 354 | (5.0) | 394 | (4.3) | 458 | (4.4) | 534 | (4.2) | 602 | (4.3) | 655 | (4.3) | 685 | (4.6) |
| Belgium | 308 | (9.4) | 354 | (8.7) | 437 | (6.7) | 523 | (3.5) | 587 | (2.3) | 634 | (2.5) | 659 | (2.4) |
| Finland | 390 | (6.1) | 429 | (5.0) | 492 | (3.0) | 553 | (2.4) | 608 | (2.5) | 654 | (2.7) | 681 | (3.4) |
| Mexico | 284 | (4.3) | 311 | (3.4) | 360 | (3.6) | 420 | (4.1) | 482 | (4.7) | 535 | (5.5) | 565 | (6.0) |
| Sweden | 353 | (4.6) | 391 | (4.1) | 456 | (3.0) | 523 | (2.4) | 581 | (2.8) | 630 | (2.8) | 657 | (3.0) |
| Switzerland | 316 | (5.5) | 355 | (5.3) | 426 | (5.5) | 503 | (4.6) | 567 | (4.6) | 621 | (5.2) | 651 | (5.3) |
| Newfoundland | 348 | (6.8) | 381 | (6.5) | 451 | (4.5) | 519 | (4.7) | 586 | (4.7) | 638 | (6.3) | 668 | (9.3) |
| Prince Edward Island | 354 | (6.1) | 391 | (8.9) | 450 | (6.0) | 521 | (5.1) | 589 | (4.6) | 641 | (4.9) | 670 | (7.2) |
| Nova Scotia | 352 | (6.8) | 391 | (5.9) | 453 | (4.9) | 521 | (3.6) | 588 | (4.2) | 641 | (6.9) | 668 | (6.7) |
| New Brunswick | 330 | (5.7) | 370 | (6.2) | 438 | (3.7) | 505 | (3.2) | 568 | (3.3) | 622 | (3.8) | 651 | (5.4) |
| Quebec | 377 | (9.1) | 414 | (6.1) | 481 | (4.6) | 546 | (3.6) | 603 | (3.4) | 651 | (2.9) | 679 | (5.6) |
| Ontario | 365 | (7.3) | 405 | (5.8) | 469 | (4.8) | 540 | (4.0) | 601 | (3.7) | 653 | (4.9) | 682 | (6.9) |
| Manitoba | 369 | (6.2) | 406 | (6.4) | 470 | (5.4) | 537 | (5.3) | 600 | (5.7) | 654 | (5.8) | 685 | (6.8) |
| Saskatchewan | 373 | (8.3) | 410 | (6.0) | 467 | (4.4) | 531 | (4.6) | 591 | (3.5) | 641 | (4.7) | 672 | (6.3) |
| Alberta | 381 | (9.2) | 423 | (7.0) | 489 | (4.9) | 557 | (4.2) | 620 | (4.7) | 672 | (5.5) | 702 | (6.2) |
| British Columbia | 373 | (7.2) | 410 | (5.5) | 473 | (3.9) | 546 | (3.7) | 605 | (3.2) | 657 | (4.3) | 687 | (6.1) |

Note: The standard error of the estimates is included in parentheses.

## TABLE 1.8

### Mathematics Scores at 5th, 10th, 25th, 50th, 75th, 90th and 95th Percentiles

| Country and province | 5th percentile | | 10th percentile | | 25th percentile | | 50th percentile | | 75th percentile | | 90th percentile | | 95th percentile | |
|---|---|---|---|---|---|---|---|---|---|---|---|---|---|---|
| **CANADA** | **390** | **(3.3)** | **423** | **(2.5)** | **476** | **(2.1)** | **536** | **(1.8)** | **592** | **(1.7)** | **640** | **(2.0)** | **668** | **(2.6)** |
| France | 364 | (6.4) | 399 | (5.1) | 457 | (4.2) | 522 | (3.1) | 581 | (3.0) | 629 | (3.2) | 656 | (4.5) |
| United States | 327 | (10.8) | 361 | (10.1) | 427 | (9.7) | 497 | (8.6) | 562 | (7.5) | 620 | (7.9) | 652 | (7.4) |
| United Kingdom | 374 | (5.4) | 412 | (3.9) | 470 | (3.4) | 532 | (2.8) | 592 | (3.1) | 646 | (4.1) | 676 | (5.5) |
| Germany | 311 | (8.0) | 349 | (6.2) | 422 | (3.9) | 497 | (4.0) | 563 | (2.7) | 619 | (3.6) | 649 | (4.1) |
| Japan | 402 | (11.5) | 440 | (9.4) | 504 | (7.4) | 563 | (5.4) | 617 | (5.2) | 662 | (5.2) | 688 | (6.3) |
| Italy | 301 | (7.8) | 338 | (5.0) | 398 | (3.2) | 462 | (3.5) | 520 | (3.6) | 570 | (4.3) | 600 | (6.1) |
| Russian Federation | 305 | (9.1) | 343 | (7.4) | 407 | (6.5) | 478 | (5.9) | 551 | (6.4) | 613 | (6.8) | 647 | (7.9) |
| Australia | 380 | (6.2) | 418 | (5.9) | 474 | (4.4) | 536 | (4.3) | 594 | (4.2) | 647 | (5.4) | 678 | (5.3) |
| Belgium | 322 | (10.1) | 367 | (8.9) | 453 | (6.7) | 533 | (4.1) | 597 | (3.0) | 646 | (3.8) | 672 | (3.8) |
| Finland | 400 | (6.4) | 433 | (3.6) | 484 | (4.0) | 538 | (2.3) | 592 | (2.4) | 636 | (3.1) | 664 | (3.8) |
| Mexico | 254 | (5.0) | 281 | (3.7) | 329 | (3.7) | 386 | (4.2) | 445 | (5.1) | 496 | (5.6) | 527 | (6.4) |
| Sweden | 347 | (5.9) | 386 | (4.4) | 450 | (3.3) | 514 | (3.0) | 574 | (2.8) | 626 | (3.3) | 656 | (4.5) |
| Switzerland | 353 | (9.2) | 398 | (6.2) | 466 | (5.0) | 535 | (5.1) | 601 | (5.2) | 653 | (5.6) | 682 | (4.9) |
| Newfoundland | 375 | (8.0) | 405 | (5.2) | 456 | (4.3) | 511 | (3.5) | 565 | (4.2) | 610 | (5.2) | 639 | (7.6) |
| Prince Edward Island | 372 | (6.8) | 405 | (5.4) | 456 | (5.6) | 516 | (4.2) | 568 | (6.0) | 614 | (6.5) | 641 | (6.1) |
| Nova Scotia | 373 | (8.2) | 403 | (5.1) | 456 | (3.8) | 513 | (3.5) | 570 | (4.1) | 621 | (4.9) | 646 | (5.1) |
| New Brunswick | 372 | (6.7) | 401 | (4.1) | 453 | (4.0) | 508 | (3.4) | 562 | (3.2) | 607 | (4.0) | 636 | (6.0) |
| Quebec | 407 | (6.9) | 443 | (5.3) | 496 | (3.8) | 554 | (3.1) | 608 | (3.3) | 654 | (3.4) | 680 | (4.4) |
| Ontario | 383 | (6.9) | 416 | (4.7) | 467 | (3.9) | 526 | (3.6) | 581 | (3.6) | 629 | (4.4) | 657 | (6.3) |
| Manitoba | 393 | (8.9) | 422 | (5.3) | 478 | (5.2) | 536 | (4.1) | 591 | (4.9) | 640 | (5.5) | 668 | (5.8) |
| Saskatchewan | 394 | (6.7) | 425 | (6.2) | 473 | (4.1) | 525 | (3.8) | 577 | (3.6) | 625 | (4.5) | 653 | (5.9) |
| Alberta | 402 | (8.0) | 437 | (6.5) | 490 | (4.1) | 550 | (4.0) | 607 | (4.5) | 656 | (5.2) | 680 | (5.9) |
| British Columbia | 390 | (5.8) | 422 | (5.4) | 477 | (4.6) | 537 | (4.3) | 594 | (3.1) | 642 | (4.3) | 669 | (5.1) |

## TABLE 1.9

### Science Scores at 5th, 10th, 25th, 50th, 75th, 90th and 95th Percentiles

| Country and province | 5th percentile | | 10th percentile | | 25th percentile | | 50th percentile | | 75th percentile | | 90th percentile | | 95th percentile | |
|---|---|---|---|---|---|---|---|---|---|---|---|---|---|---|
| **CANADA** | **380** | **(3.8)** | **412** | **(3.2)** | **469** | **(2.1)** | **532** | **(1.8)** | **592** | **(1.8)** | **641** | **(2.1)** | **670** | **(2.9)** |
| France | 329 | (6.0) | 363 | (5.2) | 429 | (5.1) | 503 | (4.1) | 575 | (3.8) | 631 | (4.0) | 662 | (4.7) |
| United States | 330 | (11.9) | 368 | (9.9) | 430 | (9.0) | 502 | (8.2) | 571 | (7.4) | 628 | (7.1) | 658 | (7.7) |
| United Kingdom | 365 | (6.8) | 401 | (6.0) | 466 | (3.6) | 535 | (3.1) | 602 | (3.8) | 656 | (4.7) | 687 | (4.9) |
| Germany | 314 | (9.0) | 350 | (5.5) | 417 | (4.7) | 491 | (4.0) | 560 | (3.1) | 618 | (3.4) | 649 | (4.5) |
| Japan | 391 | (11.1) | 430 | (10.2) | 495 | (7.5) | 557 | (5.5) | 612 | (5.1) | 659 | (4.8) | 688 | (5.8) |
| Italy | 315 | (7.1) | 349 | (5.9) | 411 | (4.3) | 480 | (3.7) | 547 | (3.6) | 602 | (3.7) | 633 | (4.6) |
| Russian Federation | 298 | (7.1) | 333 | (5.4) | 391 | (5.9) | 459 | (5.1) | 529 | (5.4) | 591 | (6.0) | 624 | (6.2) |
| Australia | 368 | (5.0) | 402 | (5.1) | 463 | (4.7) | 531 | (4.7) | 595 | (4.8) | 646 | (5.0) | 675 | (4.9) |
| Belgium | 292 | (14.1) | 346 | (10.4) | 423 | (6.3) | 507 | (4.1) | 577 | (3.6) | 630 | (2.7) | 656 | (2.9) |
| Finland | 391 | (5.1) | 425 | (3.8) | 480 | (3.5) | 540 | (2.9) | 598 | (2.8) | 645 | (3.9) | 674 | (4.1) |
| Mexico | 302 | (4.9) | 325 | (4.8) | 368 | (3.1) | 417 | (3.5) | 472 | (4.5) | 525 | (5.9) | 554 | (6.4) |
| Sweden | 357 | (5.7) | 390 | (4.4) | 446 | (3.8) | 517 | (3.3) | 578 | (3.0) | 629 | (3.2) | 659 | (4.1) |
| Switzerland | 331 | (5.7) | 365 | (5.3) | 427 | (5.0) | 496 | (5.1) | 567 | (6.2) | 625 | (6.1) | 656 | (8.2) |
| Newfoundland | 372 | (7.6) | 401 | (6.2) | 458 | (4.0) | 516 | (4.1) | 578 | (5.3) | 630 | (6.7) | 656 | (8.1) |
| Prince Edward Island | 373 | (8.4) | 400 | (5.6) | 449 | (4.2) | 505 | (4.4) | 566 | (4.2) | 619 | (5.2) | 652 | (6.4) |
| Nova Scotia | 373 | (4.9) | 401 | (4.4) | 457 | (4.4) | 518 | (4.4) | 577 | (3.9) | 624 | (4.9) | 653 | (8.8) |
| New Brunswick | 357 | (4.6) | 386 | (4.6) | 437 | (3.1) | 494 | (2.9) | 559 | (4.5) | 611 | (4.3) | 639 | (4.6) |
| Quebec | 384 | (6.6) | 418 | (5.4) | 480 | (4.4) | 546 | (3.3) | 604 | (3.6) | 653 | (4.6) | 682 | (5.6) |
| Ontario | 375 | (7.0) | 406 | (6.2) | 463 | (4.5) | 524 | (4.0) | 583 | (3.5) | 632 | (4.9) | 661 | (7.1) |
| Manitoba | 379 | (7.0) | 412 | (6.3) | 468 | (5.6) | 529 | (3.9) | 588 | (5.2) | 638 | (5.5) | 665 | (6.1) |
| Saskatchewan | 385 | (7.0) | 412 | (5.1) | 463 | (3.9) | 523 | (5.0) | 581 | (3.5) | 626 | (4.9) | 653 | (5.7) |
| Alberta | 395 | (8.8) | 429 | (7.3) | 487 | (4.8) | 548 | (4.4) | 610 | (3.9) | 656 | (4.9) | 685 | (7.5) |
| British Columbia | 386 | (7.1) | 418 | (5.2) | 471 | (4.2) | 536 | (3.8) | 597 | (4.0) | 642 | (4.0) | 670 | (4.8) |

| TABLE 1.10 | TABLE 1.11 |
|---|---|

### Reading Inequality Index (90th percentile/10th percentile)

| Country and province | Inequality index |
|---|---|
| **CANADA** | **1.59** |
| France | 1.62 |
| United States | 1.75 |
| United Kingdom | 1.67 |
| Germany | 1.85 |
| Japan | 1.54 |
| Italy | 1.64 |
| Russian Federation | 1.70 |
| Australia | 1.66 |
| Belgium | 1.79 |
| Finland | 1.52 |
| Mexico | 1.72 |
| Sweden | 1.61 |
| Switzerland | 1.75 |
| Newfoundland | 1.67 |
| Prince Edward Island | 1.64 |
| Nova Scotia | 1.64 |
| New Brunswick | 1.68 |
| Quebec | 1.57 |
| Ontario | 1.61 |
| Manitoba | 1.61 |
| Saskatchewan | 1.57 |
| Alberta | 1.59 |
| British Columbia | 1.60 |

### Mathematics Inequality Index (90th percentile/10th percentile)

| Country and province | Inequality index |
|---|---|
| **CANADA** | **1.51** |
| France | 1.58 |
| United States | 1.72 |
| United Kingdom | 1.57 |
| Germany | 1.78 |
| Japan | 1.50 |
| Italy | 1.68 |
| Russian Federation | 1.79 |
| Australia | 1.55 |
| Belgium | 1.76 |
| Finland | 1.47 |
| Mexico | 1.77 |
| Sweden | 1.62 |
| Switzerland | 1.64 |
| Newfoundland | 1.51 |
| Prince Edward Island | 1.51 |
| Nova Scotia | 1.54 |
| New Brunswick | 1.51 |
| Quebec | 1.47 |
| Ontario | 1.51 |
| Manitoba | 1.51 |
| Saskatchewan | 1.47 |
| Alberta | 1.50 |
| British Columbia | 1.52 |

| TABLE 1.12 |
|---|

### Science Inequality Index (90th percentile/10th percentile)

| Country and province | Inequality index |
|---|---|
| **CANADA** | **1.56** |
| France | 1.74 |
| United States | 1.71 |
| United Kingdom | 1.63 |
| Germany | 1.77 |
| Japan | 1.53 |
| Italy | 1.73 |
| Russian Federation | 1.77 |
| Australia | 1.61 |
| Belgium | 1.82 |
| Finland | 1.52 |
| Mexico | 1.61 |
| Sweden | 1.62 |
| Switzerland | 1.71 |
| Newfoundland | 1.57 |
| Prince Edward Island | 1.55 |
| Nova Scotia | 1.55 |
| New Brunswick | 1.58 |
| Quebec | 1.56 |
| Ontario | 1.56 |
| Manitoba | 1.55 |
| Saskatchewan | 1.52 |
| Alberta | 1.53 |
| British Columbia | 1.54 |

## TABLE 1.13

### Percent of Students Above 50th, 75th and 90th International Percentile: READING

| Country and province | 50th percentile | 75th percentile | 90th percentile |
|---|---|---|---|
| Alberta | 71 | 46 | 24 |
| Finland | 73 | 45 | 20 |
| British Columbia | 67 | 42 | 20 |
| Australia | 63 | 38 | 19 |
| **CANADA** | **66** | **39** | **18** |
| Ontario | 66 | 39 | 18 |
| Manitoba | 64 | 36 | 17 |
| Quebec | 68 | 40 | 17 |
| United Kingdom | 61 | 36 | 17 |
| Saskatchewan | 65 | 36 | 15 |
| Nova Scotia | 61 | 34 | 15 |
| Newfoundland | 58 | 32 | 15 |
| Prince Edward Island | 58 | 33 | 14 |
| Belgium | 59 | 34 | 14 |
| United States | 55 | 29 | 13 |
| Sweden | 60 | 32 | 13 |
| Japan | 65 | 33 | 11 |
| New Brunswick | 53 | 26 | 10 |
| Switzerland | 52 | 26 | 10 |
| Germany | 49 | 24 | 10 |
| France | 55 | 27 | 10 |
| Italy | 48 | 21 | 6 |
| Russian Federation | 36 | 13 | 4 |
| Mexico | 20 | 5 | 1 |

## TABLE 1.14

### Percent of Students Above 50th, 75th and 90th International Percentile: MATHEMATICS

| Country and province | 50th percentile | 75th percentile | 90th percentile |
|---|---|---|---|
| Japan | 76 | 47 | 21 |
| Alberta | 71 | 41 | 18 |
| Quebec | 74 | 43 | 18 |
| Switzerland | 63 | 36 | 17 |
| Belgium | 62 | 35 | 15 |
| Australia | 66 | 35 | 15 |
| United Kingdom | 64 | 34 | 14 |
| British Columbia | 66 | 36 | 14 |
| Manitoba | 67 | 34 | 13 |
| **CANADA** | **66** | **35** | **13** |
| Finland | 69 | 35 | 12 |
| France | 59 | 30 | 11 |
| Ontario | 62 | 31 | 10 |
| Saskatchewan | 63 | 29 | 10 |
| Sweden | 56 | 27 | 10 |
| United States | 49 | 23 | 9 |
| Nova Scotia | 57 | 26 | 9 |
| Germany | 49 | 23 | 8 |
| Russian Federation | 42 | 20 | 8 |
| Prince Edward Island | 57 | 25 | 7 |
| Newfoundland | 56 | 23 | 6 |
| New Brunswick | 54 | 22 | 6 |
| Italy | 34 | 10 | 2 |
| Mexico | 9 | 1 | 0 |

## TABLE 1.15

### Percent of Students Above 50th, 75th and 90th International Percentile: SCIENCE

| Country and province | 50th percentile | 75th percentile | 90th percentile | Country and province | 50th percentile | 75th percentile | 90th percentile |
|---|---|---|---|---|---|---|---|
| Japan | 75 | 45 | 20 | Newfoundland | 59 | 28 | 11 |
| Alberta | 72 | 42 | 19 | Sweden | 58 | 29 | 11 |
| United Kingdom | 65 | 37 | 17 | United States | 52 | 26 | 10 |
| Quebec | 70 | 40 | 17 | Saskatchewan | 62 | 30 | 10 |
| Finland | 69 | 38 | 15 | Switzerland | 50 | 25 | 10 |
| Australia | 63 | 35 | 15 | Nova Scotia | 60 | 28 | 9 |
| British Columbia | 66 | 36 | 14 | Prince Edward Island | 54 | 24 | 9 |
| **CANADA** | **65** | **35** | **14** | Germany | 48 | 22 | 8 |
| | | | | New Brunswick | 49 | 21 | 7 |
| Manitoba | 64 | 33 | 13 | Italy | 43 | 18 | 6 |
| Ontario | 62 | 31 | 11 | Russian Federation | 36 | 15 | 5 |
| Belgium | 54 | 28 | 11 | Mexico | 17 | 4 | 1 |
| France | 52 | 27 | 11 | | | | |

Note:  Tables 1.13 to 1.15 represent the proportion of students in each jurisdiction at or above the score representing the 50th, 75th and 90th percentiles for students in the 14 countries combined.

## TABLE 1.16

### Reading Proficiency Scales: Percent of Students at Each Level

| Country and province | Below Level 1 | | Level 1 | | Level 2 | | Level 3 | | Level 4 | | Level 5 | |
|---|---|---|---|---|---|---|---|---|---|---|---|---|
| **CANADA** | **2.4** | **(0.3)** | **7.3** | **(0.3)** | **17.9** | **(0.4)** | **28.0** | **(0.5)** | **27.7** | **(0.6)** | **16.8** | **(0.5)** |
| France | 4.2 | (0.6) | 11.1 | (0.8) | 21.9 | (0.8) | 30.6 | (1.0) | 23.7 | (0.9) | 8.5 | (0.5) |
| United States | 6.4 | (1.2) | 11.6 | (1.2) | 21.6 | (1.2) | 27.4 | (1.3) | 20.7 | (1.2) | 12.3 | (1.3) |
| United Kingdom | 3.6 | (0.4) | 9.3 | (0.5) | 19.6 | (0.7) | 27.5 | (0.9) | 24.4 | (0.9) | 15.6 | (0.9) |
| Germany | 9.9 | (0.7) | 12.8 | (0.6) | 22.2 | (0.8) | 26.8 | (1.0) | 19.4 | (1.0) | 8.8 | (0.5) |
| Japan | 2.7 | (0.6) | 7.4 | (1.1) | 17.9 | (1.2) | 33.3 | (1.3) | 28.8 | (1.7) | 9.9 | (1.1) |
| Italy | 5.3 | (0.7) | 13.7 | (0.9) | 25.5 | (1.0) | 30.6 | (1.0) | 19.5 | (1.1) | 5.5 | (0.7) |
| Russian Federation | 9.0 | (1.0) | 18.6 | (1.1) | 29.1 | (0.9) | 26.9 | (1.1) | 13.2 | (1.0) | 3.2 | (0.5) |
| Australia | 3.3 | (0.5) | 9.2 | (0.7) | 18.9 | (1.1) | 25.2 | (0.8) | 25.8 | (1.0) | 17.6 | (1.2) |
| Belgium | 7.7 | (1.0) | 11.4 | (0.8) | 16.7 | (0.7) | 25.7 | (0.8) | 26.5 | (0.8) | 12.0 | (0.7) |
| Finland | 1.7 | (0.5) | 5.3 | (0.4) | 14.2 | (0.7) | 28.7 | (0.8) | 31.6 | (0.9) | 18.5 | (0.9) |
| Mexico | 16.1 | (1.2) | 28.3 | (1.4) | 30.0 | (1.1) | 18.8 | (1.2) | 6.0 | (0.7) | 0.9 | (0.2) |
| Sweden | 3.3 | (0.4) | 9.3 | (0.6) | 20.2 | (0.7) | 30.4 | (1.0) | 25.5 | (1.0) | 11.2 | (0.7) |
| Switzerland | 7.0 | (0.7) | 13.4 | (0.9) | 21.5 | (1.0) | 28.0 | (1.0) | 20.9 | (0.9) | 9.2 | (1.0) |
| Newfoundland | 3.5 | (0.5) | 10.3 | (0.9) | 21.0 | (1.3) | 28.4 | (1.4) | 23.5 | (1.2) | 13.3 | (0.9) |
| Prince Edward Island | 2.4 | (0.5) | 10.4 | (1.2) | 21.9 | (1.2) | 28.3 | (1.5) | 23.9 | (1.6) | 13.1 | (1.1) |
| Nova Scotia | 2.9 | (0.4) | 9.2 | (0.9) | 20.7 | (1.2) | 29.0 | (1.3) | 24.6 | (1.5) | 13.6 | (0.9) |
| New Brunswick | 5.1 | (0.5) | 11.7 | (0.8) | 23.1 | (1.2) | 29.7 | (1.1) | 21.0 | (1.0) | 9.5 | (0.6) |
| Quebec | 2.0 | (0.4) | 6.4 | (0.6) | 17.2 | (0.9) | 29.4 | (1.1) | 29.2 | (1.1) | 15.9 | (1.0) |
| Ontario | 2.6 | (0.6) | 7.4 | (0.6) | 18.2 | (0.8) | 27.5 | (0.9) | 27.6 | (1.1) | 16.7 | (1.0) |
| Manitoba | 2.0 | (0.4) | 8.6 | (0.9) | 18.7 | (1.2) | 29.6 | (1.5) | 25.2 | (1.2) | 15.9 | (1.2) |
| Saskatchewan | 2.0 | (0.5) | 7.3 | (0.5) | 19.2 | (0.9) | 29.8 | (1.3) | 27.8 | (1.1) | 14.0 | (1.0) |
| Alberta | 1.8 | (0.5) | 6.1 | (0.7) | 14.7 | (0.8) | 26.7 | (1.2) | 28.2 | (1.0) | 22.5 | (1.4) |
| British Columbia | 2.4 | (0.5) | 7.0 | (0.7) | 17.5 | (0.9) | 26.3 | (1.1) | 28.7 | (1.0) | 18.1 | (1.1) |

Note: The standard error of the estimates is included in parenthesis.

## TABLE 1.17

### Average Reading Scores by Gender

| Country and province | Girls | | | | Boys | | |
|---|---|---|---|---|---|---|---|
| | Average | Standard error | Confidence interval (+ -) | | Average | Standard error | Confidence interval (+ -) |
| **CANADA** | 551 | (1.7) | 3.4 | | 519 | (1.8) | 3.5 |
| France | **519** | (2.7) | 5.4 | | **490** | (3.5) | 7.0 |
| United States* | **518** | (6.2) | 12.3 | | **490** | (8.4) | 16.7 |
| United Kingdom | **537** | (3.4) | 6.9 | | **512** | (3.0) | 6.0 |
| Germany | **502** | (3.9) | 7.7 | | **468** | (3.2) | 6.3 |
| Japan | **537** | (5.4) | 10.7 | | **507** | (6.7) | 13.4 |
| Italy | **507** | (3.6) | 7.1 | | **469** | (5.1) | 10.2 |
| Russian Federation | **481** | (4.1) | 8.1 | | **443** | (4.5) | 9.0 |
| Australia | **546** | (4.7) | 9.4 | | **513** | (4.0) | 8.0 |
| Belgium | **525** | (4.9) | 9.8 | | **492** | (4.2) | 8.4 |
| Finland | **571** | (2.8) | 5.5 | | **520** | (3.0) | 6.0 |
| Mexico | **432** | (3.8) | 7.6 | | **411** | (4.2) | 8.3 |
| Sweden | **536** | (2.5) | 4.9 | | **499** | (2.6) | 5.1 |
| Switzerland | **510** | (4.5) | 9.0 | | **480** | (4.9) | 9.7 |
| Newfoundland | 538 | (3.1) | 6.1 | | 496 | (3.7) | 7.4 |
| Prince Edward Island | 535 | (3.5) | 7.0 | | 500 | (3.0) | 6.0 |
| Nova Scotia | 538 | (3.1) | 6.1 | | 505 | (3.4) | 6.7 |
| New Brunswick | 525 | (2.0) | 4.1 | | 478 | (2.7) | 5.5 |
| Quebec | 553 | (3.3) | 6.5 | | 521 | (3.4) | 6.8 |
| Ontario | 548 | (3.5) | 6.9 | | 518 | (3.9) | 7.8 |
| Manitoba | 548 | (4.2) | 8.4 | | 513 | (3.7) | 7.4 |
| Saskatchewan | 548 | (3.3) | 6.6 | | 512 | (3.2) | 6.4 |
| Alberta | 571 | (3.5) | 7.1 | | 533 | (4.0) | 7.9 |
| British Columbia | 555 | (3.3) | 6.6 | | 523 | (4.0) | 7.9 |

Note: Average scores are bolded for jurisdictions where there are significant differences between girls and boys.

* Although the confidence interval overlaps by one point, the difference in mean scores is significant at the 95% level.

## TABLE 1.18

### Average Mathematics Scores by Gender

| Country and province | Girls | | | Boys | | |
|---|---|---|---|---|---|---|
| | Average | Standard error | Confidence interval (+ -) | Average | Standard error | Confidence interval (+ -) |
| CANADA | 529 | (1.6) | 3.2 | 539 | (1.8) | 3.5 |
| France | **511** | (2.8) | 5.6 | **525** | (4.1) | 8.1 |
| United States | 490 | (7.3) | 14.6 | 497 | (8.9) | 17.6 |
| United Kingdom | 526 | (3.7) | 7.3 | 534 | (3.5) | 6.9 |
| Germany | **483** | (4.0) | 8.0 | **498** | (3.1) | 6.2 |
| Japan | 553 | (5.9) | 11.8 | 561 | (7.3) | 14.5 |
| Italy | 454 | (3.8) | 7.5 | 462 | (5.3) | 10.6 |
| Russian Federation | 479 | (6.2) | 12.4 | 478 | (5.7) | 11.3 |
| Australia | 527 | (5.1) | 10.2 | 539 | (4.1) | 8.2 |
| Belgium | 518 | (5.2) | 10.3 | 524 | (4.6) | 9.2 |
| Finland | 536 | (2.6) | 5.2 | 537 | (2.8) | 5.6 |
| Mexico | 382 | (3.8) | 7.6 | 393 | (4.5) | 8.9 |
| Sweden | 507 | (3.0) | 6.0 | 514 | (3.2) | 6.5 |
| Switzerland | 523 | (4.8) | 9.6 | 537 | (5.3) | 10.6 |
| Newfoundland | 507 | (3.6) | 7.1 | 513 | (4.5) | 8.9 |
| Prince Edward Island | 508 | (5.0) | 9.9 | 518 | (4.5) | 9.0 |
| Nova Scotia | 507 | (3.8) | 7.5 | 520 | (4.3) | 8.6 |
| New Brunswick | 508 | (2.5) | 5.0 | 506 | (3.5) | 7.0 |
| Quebec | 547 | (3.2) | 6.3 | 556 | (3.4) | 6.7 |
| Ontario | 520 | (3.2) | 6.4 | 529 | (3.9) | 7.8 |
| Manitoba | 532 | (5.1) | 10.1 | 535 | (3.9) | 7.8 |
| Saskatchewan | 519 | (4.0) | 8.0 | 531 | (3.4) | 6.8 |
| Alberta | 543 | (3.7) | 7.4 | 553 | (4.6) | 9.1 |
| British Columbia | 528 | (4.1) | 8.1 | 541 | (3.5) | 7.0 |

Note: Average scores are bolded for jurisdictions where there are significant differences between girls and boys.

## TABLE 1.19

### Average Science Scores by Gender

| Country and province | Girls | | | Boys | | |
|---|---|---|---|---|---|---|
| | Average | Standard error | Confidence interval (+ -) | Average | Standard error | Confidence interval (+ -) |
| **CANADA** | **531** | **(1.7)** | **3.5** | **529** | **(1.9)** | **3.8** |
| France | 498 | (3.8) | 7.5 | 504 | (4.2) | 8.4 |
| United States | 502 | (6.5) | 12.9 | 497 | (8.9) | 17.8 |
| United Kingdom | 531 | (4.0) | 7.9 | 535 | (3.4) | 6.8 |
| Germany | 487 | (3.4) | 6.8 | 489 | (3.4) | 6.7 |
| Japan | 554 | (5.9) | 11.7 | 547 | (7.2) | 14.3 |
| Italy | 483 | (3.9) | 7.8 | 474 | (5.6) | 11.2 |
| Russian Federation | 467 | (5.2) | 10.3 | 453 | (5.4) | 10.7 |
| Australia | 529 | (4.8) | 9.5 | 526 | (3.9) | 7.8 |
| Belgium | 498 | (5.6) | 11.2 | 496 | (5.2) | 10.4 |
| Finland | 541 | (2.7) | 5.4 | 534 | (3.5) | 7.0 |
| Mexico | 419 | (3.9) | 7.7 | 423 | (4.2) | 8.4 |
| Sweden | 513 | (2.9) | 5.7 | 512 | (3.5) | 6.9 |
| Switzerland | 493 | (4.7) | 9.3 | 500 | (5.7) | 11.3 |
| Newfoundland | 522 | (4.6) | 9.1 | 511 | (4.7) | 9.3 |
| Prince Edward Island | 511 | (3.7) | 7.3 | 506 | (4.2) | 8.3 |
| Nova Scotia | 518 | (4.2) | 8.4 | 515 | (4.5) | 9.0 |
| New Brunswick | 505 | (3.1) | 6.1 | 490 | (3.2) | 6.4 |
| Quebec | 542 | (4.1) | 8.2 | 541 | (3.8) | 7.6 |
| Ontario | 525 | (3.6) | 7.2 | 520 | (4.5) | 8.9 |
| Manitoba | 526 | (4.4) | 8.8 | 530 | (4.4) | 8.7 |
| Saskatchewan | 521 | (4.1) | 8.1 | 523 | (3.5) | 7.1 |
| Alberta | 549 | (3.8) | 7.6 | 545 | (4.5) | 8.9 |
| British Columbia | 533 | (3.9) | 7.8 | 535 | (4.3) | 8.5 |

## TABLE 1.20

### Average Scores by Province and Language of the School System

| Province | Reading | | | | | | Science | | | | | |
|---|---|---|---|---|---|---|---|---|---|---|---|---|
| | Anglophone average | Standard error | Confidence interval (+ -) | Francophone average | Standard error | Confidence interval (+ -) | Anglophone average | Standard error | Confidence interval (+ -) | Francophone average | Standard error | Confidence interval (+ -) |
| Nova Scotia | **522** | (2.3) | 4.7 | **474** | (5.2) | 10.4 | **517** | (3.0) | 6.1 | **466** | (8.2) | 16.4 |
| New Brunswick | **512** | (2.3) | 4.6 | **478** | (2.6) | 5.1 | **503** | (2.9) | 5.8 | **483** | (3.8) | 7.5 |
| Quebec | 543 | (4.6) | 9.1 | 535 | (3.3) | 6.6 | 531 | (5.0) | 9.9 | 542 | (3.8) | 7.5 |
| Ontario | **535** | (3.4) | 6.7 | **474** | (7.4) | 14.7 | **524** | (3.6) | 7.1 | **479** | (7.3) | 14.6 |
| Manitoba | **530** | (3.6) | 7.1 | **486** | (5.5) | 10.9 | **527** | (3.6) | 7.2 | **500** | (8.5) | 17.0 |

| Province | Mathematics | | | | | |
|---|---|---|---|---|---|---|
| | Anglophone average | Standard error | Confidence interval (+ -) | Francophone average | Standard error | Confidence interval (+ -) |
| Nova Scotia | 513 | (2.9) | 5.7 | 508 | (6.5) | 12.9 |
| New Brunswick | 505 | (2.7) | 5.3 | 509 | (3.7) | 7.5 |
| Quebec | 544 | (4.2) | 8.4 | 551 | (3.0) | 5.9 |
| Ontario | **525** | (3.0) | 6.0 | **497** | (7.5) | 14.9 |
| Manitoba | 534 | (3.7) | 7.4 | 517 | (7.2) | 14.3 |

Note: Average scores are bolded for jurisdictions where there are significant differences between anglophone and francophone school systems.

## TABLE 2.1

### Effects of Reading Enjoyment and Reading Diversity on Achievement Scores in Reading

| Country and province | Standardized Effect | | Country and province | Standardized Effect | |
|---|---|---|---|---|---|
| | Reading enjoyment | Reading diversity | | Reading enjoyment | Reading diversity |
| **CANADA** | **0.42** | **0.23** | Sweden | 0.44 | 0.32 |
| | | | Switzerland | 0.40 | 0.36 |
| France | 0.30 | 0.29 | Newfoundland | 0.46 | 0.29 |
| United States | 0.32 | 0.23 | Prince Edward Island | 0.45 | 0.27 |
| United Kingdom | 0.38 | 0.23 | Nova Scotia | 0.48 | 0.31 |
| Germany | 0.40 | 0.29 | New Brunswick | 0.46 | 0.32 |
| Japan | 0.30 | 0.26 | Quebec | 0.37 | 0.24 |
| Italy | 0.30 | 0.19 | Ontario | 0.42 | 0.21 |
| Russian Federation | 0.30 | 0.09 | Manitoba | 0.46 | 0.22 |
| Australia | 0.42 | 0.27 | Saskatchewan | 0.44 | 0.22 |
| Belgium | 0.30 | 0.34 | Alberta | 0.45 | 0.21 |
| Finland | 0.47 | 0.35 | British Columbia | 0.44 | 0.23 |
| Mexico | 0.13 | 0.29 | | | |

## TABLE 2.2

### Average Achievement Scores in Reading by Time Spent Reading for Enjoyment

| Country and province | Don't read | Standard error | 30 minutes or less | Standard error | 31–60 minutes | Standard error | 1–2 hours | Standard error | More than 2 hours | Standard error |
|---|---|---|---|---|---|---|---|---|---|---|
| **CANADA** | **498** | **(1.6)** | **544** | **(1.8)** | **564** | **(2.1)** | **575** | **(3.4)** | **550** | **(4.9)** |
| France | 472 | (3.4) | 519 | (2.9) | 533 | (3.1) | 539 | (4.3) | 514 | (10.0) |
| United States | 479 | (7.0) | 530 | (7.3) | 531 | (8.4) | 539 | (12.2) | 511 | (10.8) |
| United Kingdom | 485 | (3.0) | 533 | (3.1) | 559 | (3.5) | 556 | (5.6) | 528 | (9.8) |
| Germany | 459 | (3.0) | 518 | (3.6) | 532 | (3.9) | 543 | (4.4) | 501 | (7.4) |
| Japan | 514 | (5.2) | 539 | (5.5) | 537 | (6.4) | 541 | (6.4) | 530 | (8.8) |
| Italy | 461 | (3.7) | 498 | (3.3) | 509 | (3.6) | 502 | (4.7) | 509 | (9.6) |
| Russian Federation | 434 | (5.9) | 455 | (5.2) | 473 | (4.2) | 483 | (3.6) | 481 | (5.4) |
| Australia | 484 | (3.9) | 537 | (3.9) | 564 | (4.7) | 575 | (5.5) | 558 | (9.8) |
| Belgium | 487 | (3.4) | 534 | (4.1) | 541 | (4.1) | 546 | (6.5) | 511 | (12.1) |
| Finland | 498 | (3.4) | 542 | (3.2) | 568 | (3.2) | 577 | (4.1) | 584 | (6.0) |
| Mexico | 420 | (6.0) | 423 | (3.6) | 439 | (3.9) | 426 | (5.4) | 407 | (7.6) |
| Sweden | 483 | (2.8) | 527 | (3.6) | 547 | (3.1) | 556 | (4.9) | 529 | (8.8) |
| Switzerland | 450 | (4.1) | 515 | (4.8) | 533 | (4.7) | 533 | (7.8) | 499 | (12.8) |
| Newfoundland | 478 | (3.7) | 524 | (3.9) | 552 | (6.0) | 573 | (7.4) | 567 | (14.8) |
| Prince Edward Island | 475 | (3.8) | 531 | (3.8) | 555 | (5.4) | 565 | (8.1) | 547 | (13.9) |
| Nova Scotia | 474 | (3.4) | 530 | (3.7) | 561 | (4.9) | 560 | (5.5) | 568 | (8.8) |
| New Brunswick | 458 | (2.8) | 513 | (3.1) | 543 | (4.7) | 555 | (5.3) | 521 | (10.9) |
| Quebec | 505 | (3.4) | 546 | (3.2) | 573 | (4.0) | 568 | (6.8) | 539 | (7.7) |
| Ontario | 497 | (3.7) | 543 | (3.7) | 556 | (4.2) | 576 | (7.6) | 547 | (11.8) |
| Manitoba | 490 | (4.2) | 539 | (4.6) | 566 | (6.1) | 574 | (8.6) | 557 | (12.2) |
| Saskatchewan | 491 | (3.1) | 547 | (3.4) | 558 | (5.7) | 571 | (6.1) | 536 | (9.1) |
| Alberta | 510 | (4.3) | 561 | (3.9) | 583 | (4.6) | 584 | (5.5) | 580 | (11.1) |
| British Columbia | 497 | (4.3) | 545 | (3.3) | 567 | (4.1) | 582 | (5.5) | 551 | (9.0) |

## TABLE 2.3

### Average Achievement Scores in Reading, Mathematics and Science by Use of Public and School Libraries

| Country and province | Never | Standard error | Few times a year | Standard error | Once a month | Standard error | Several times a month | Standard error |
|---|---|---|---|---|---|---|---|---|
| A. READING | | | | | | | | |
| **CANADA** | 514 | (1.9) | 542 | (1.7) | 555 | (2.1) | 563 | (4.2) |
| France | 501 | (3.1) | 515 | (3.2) | 519 | (4.5) | 529 | (6.1) |
| United States | 491 | (7.0) | 518 | (8.3) | 536 | (7.1) | 525 | (11.8) |
| United Kingdom | 504 | (2.5) | 540 | (3.6) | 552 | (4.6) | 538 | (8.3) |
| Germany | 480 | (3.2) | 512 | (3.2) | 520 | (5.3) | 509 | (11.2) |
| Japan | 507 | (5.5) | 541 | (4.6) | 551 | (6.3) | 553 | (9.0) |
| Italy | 477 | (3.8) | 500 | (2.8) | 511 | (5.4) | 486 | (10.4) |
| Russian Federation | 458 | (4.4) | 467 | (5.1) | 470 | (5.2) | 458 | (3.9) |
| Australia | 500 | (4.0) | 537 | (3.8) | 559 | (5.9) | 562 | (9.3) |
| Belgium | 484 | (4.2) | 518 | (3.2) | 550 | (5.2) | 538 | (12.6) |
| Finland | 502 | (3.9) | 537 | (3.1) | 570 | (2.9) | 589 | (3.9) |
| Mexico | 426 | (5.1) | 432 | (4.0) | 420 | (4.3) | 394 | (5.2) |
| Sweden | 492 | (2.8) | 526 | (2.8) | 543 | (4.0) | 551 | (6.5) |
| Switzerland | 469 | (4.7) | 510 | (4.7) | 522 | (5.2) | 516 | (7.7) |
| Newfoundland | 505 | (3.4) | 526 | (5.0) | 547 | (8.2) | 543 | (14.1) |
| Prince Edward Island | 493 | (3.6) | 534 | (3.5) | 545 | (5.6) | 547 | (10.7) |
| Nova Scotia | 499 | (3.5) | 531 | (3.3) | 544 | (5.9) | 574 | (8.1) |
| New Brunswick | 480 | (3.2) | 514 | (3.2) | 520 | (5.1) | 541 | (6.7) |
| Quebec | 516 | (3.6) | 541 | (3.6) | 552 | (3.3) | 557 | (6.2) |
| Ontario | 515 | (4.1) | 541 | (3.6) | 554 | (4.6) | 558 | (9.5) |
| Manitoba | 506 | (4.1) | 540 | (4.5) | 553 | (5.9) | 558 | (7.2) |
| Saskatchewan | 500 | (3.1) | 540 | (3.8) | 552 | (5.2) | 566 | (6.8) |
| Alberta | 526 | (3.9) | 560 | (3.9) | 573 | (5.4) | 586 | (9.6) |
| British Columbia | 516 | (4.0) | 544 | (3.4) | 558 | (4.6) | 573 | (6.7) |
| B. MATHEMATICS | | | | | | | | |
| **CANADA** | 523 | (1.9) | 538 | (1.7) | 544 | (2.4) | 542 | (3.9) |
| France | 520 | (3.3) | 523 | (3.9) | 523 | (5.3) | 527 | (8.0) |
| United States | 490 | (8.3) | 502 | (9.5) | 512 | (8.7) | 498 | (11.9) |
| United Kingdom | 521 | (2.7) | 542 | (3.9) | 543 | (4.8) | 524 | (7.3) |
| Germany | 488 | (3.9) | 510 | (4.0) | 512 | (5.1) | 486 | (12.0) |
| Japan | 545 | (6.3) | 571 | (5.4) | 576 | (7.5) | 579 | (9.3) |
| Italy | 452 | (4.0) | 465 | (3.4) | 474 | (7.0) | 437 | (13.2) |
| Russian Federation | 476 | (6.9) | 485 | (6.0) | 486 | (8.8) | 471 | (6.3) |
| Australia | 517 | (4.3) | 541 | (4.7) | 553 | (6.4) | 547 | (7.8) |
| Belgium | 508 | (4.8) | 530 | (4.1) | 552 | (5.6) | 533 | (12.7) |
| Finland | 521 | (3.7) | 532 | (3.3) | 545 | (3.1) | 557 | (4.6) |
| Mexico | 393 | (4.7) | 398 | (4.3) | 386 | (5.1) | 354 | (5.9) |
| Sweden | 497 | (3.3) | 515 | (3.6) | 527 | (5.4) | 528 | (8.5) |
| Switzerland | 518 | (5.4) | 539 | (5.0) | 542 | (6.0) | 529 | (9.5) |
| Newfoundland | 505 | (3.5) | 519 | (5.6) | 513 | (9.8) | 505 | (12.6) |
| Prince Edward Island | 503 | (5.3) | 520 | (4.8) | 529 | (7.8) | 507 | (12.0) |
| Nova Scotia | 506 | (4.7) | 517 | (4.3) | 516 | (7.3) | 543 | (11.6) |
| New Brunswick | 499 | (3.3) | 514 | (3.6) | 514 | (6.0) | 511 | (8.6) |
| Quebec | 542 | (3.8) | 555 | (3.6) | 559 | (4.4) | 552 | (6.9) |
| Ontario | 515 | (3.8) | 529 | (3.8) | 536 | (4.9) | 529 | (8.8) |
| Manitoba | 522 | (4.7) | 540 | (5.5) | 542 | (7.1) | 549 | (8.5) |
| Saskatchewan | 515 | (3.8) | 532 | (4.7) | 525 | (5.2) | 542 | (7.2) |
| Alberta | 538 | (4.5) | 553 | (5.0) | 558 | (5.8) | 556 | (10.4) |
| British Columbia | 525 | (3.6) | 536 | (3.9) | 546 | (5.6) | 549 | (8.1) |

## TABLE 2.3 (continued)

### Average Achievement Scores in Reading, Mathematics and Science by Use of Public and School Libraries

| Country and province | Never | Standard error | Few times a year | Standard error | Once a month | Standard error | Several times a month | Standard error |
|---|---|---|---|---|---|---|---|---|
| | | | | C. SCIENCE | | | | |
| **CANADA** | **514** | **(2.4)** | **535** | **(2.0)** | **545** | **(2.7)** | **553** | **(4.2)** |
| France | 504 | (3.7) | 509 | (4.2) | 510 | (6.9) | 528 | (8.4) |
| United States | 490 | (8.2) | 511 | (9.5) | 526 | (8.4) | 525 | (10.2) |
| United Kingdom | 515 | (3.1) | 549 | (4.1) | 556 | (5.1) | 537 | (10.6) |
| Germany | 482 | (3.5) | 511 | (4.0) | 505 | (7.6) | 520 | (8.5) |
| Japan | 532 | (6.1) | 570 | (5.2) | 586 | (7.5) | 589 | (8.9) |
| Italy | 471 | (4.3) | 487 | (3.7) | 498 | (6.4) | 481 | (13.5) |
| Russian Federation | 458 | (5.3) | 466 | (6.7) | 466 | (6.5) | 457 | (5.2) |
| Australia | 507 | (4.2) | 530 | (3.7) | 554 | (6.5) | 556 | (9.7) |
| Belgium | 479 | (4.7) | 506 | (3.7) | 534 | (6.5) | 516 | (16.0) |
| Finland | 505 | (4.6) | 530 | (3.3) | 554 | (3.4) | 573 | (4.6) |
| Mexico | 425 | (5.5) | 429 | (4.2) | 419 | (4.9) | 400 | (4.7) |
| Sweden | 496 | (3.4) | 520 | (3.5) | 528 | (5.4) | 534 | (9.3) |
| Switzerland | 477 | (5.1) | 502 | (5.6) | 519 | (5.8) | 516 | (8.7) |
| Newfoundland | 508 | (4.0) | 521 | (6.6) | 542 | (8.7) | 544 | (15.4) |
| Prince Edward Island | 490 | (4.1) | 519 | (5.5) | 534 | (7.0) | 528 | (13.3) |
| Nova Scotia | 500 | (4.1) | 520 | (4.6) | 537 | (7.2) | 571 | (12.9) |
| New Brunswick | 480 | (3.9) | 507 | (3.9) | 512 | (5.9) | 527 | (9.2) |
| Quebec | 529 | (4.6) | 545 | (4.4) | 548 | (5.0) | 555 | (7.9) |
| Ontario | 507 | (4.9) | 528 | (4.2) | 538 | (5.8) | 546 | (9.3) |
| Manitoba | 511 | (4.8) | 536 | (4.5) | 546 | (5.6) | 538 | (9.6) |
| Saskatchewan | 502 | (3.7) | 532 | (4.5) | 533 | (7.2) | 549 | (8.0) |
| Alberta | 529 | (5.2) | 550 | (4.4) | 567 | (5.7) | 575 | (11.1) |
| British Columbia | 517 | (5.0) | 538 | (4.1) | 547 | (4.9) | 561 | (7.7) |

## TABLE 2.4

### Effects of Homework Time and Sense of Belonging to School on Achievement Scores in Reading, Mathematics and Science

| Country and province | Standardized Effect | | Country and province | Standardized Effect | |
|---|---|---|---|---|---|
| | Homework time | Sense of belonging to school | | Homework time | Sense of belonging to school |
| **A. READING** | | | **C. SCIENCE** | | |
| **CANADA** | **0.24** | **0.04** | **CANADA** | **0.17** | **0.01** |
| France | 0.34 | 0.06 | France | 0.29 | 0.03 |
| United States | 0.31 | 0.11 | United States | 0.27 | 0.11 |
| United Kingdom | 0.30 | 0.06 | United Kingdom | 0.28 | 0.06 |
| Germany | 0.11 | 0.08 | Germany | 0.05 | 0.05 |
| Japan | 0.31 | 0.09 | Japan | 0.34 | 0.03 |
| Italy | 0.24 | -0.01 | Italy | 0.23 | -0.02 |
| Russian Federation | 0.30 | 0.13 | Russian Federation | 0.27 | 0.11 |
| Australia | 0.28 | 0.04 | Australia | 0.29 | -0.02 |
| Belgium | 0.32 | 0.08 | Belgium | 0.27 | 0.06 |
| Finland | 0.17 | -0.03 | Finland | 0.12 | -0.02 |
| Mexico | 0.14 | 0.24 | Mexico | 0.14 | 0.17 |
| Sweden | 0.05 | -0.02 | Sweden | 0.02 | -0.02 |
| Switzerland | 0.02 | 0.13 | Switzerland | 0.01 | 0.09 |
| Newfoundland | 0.17 | 0.07 | Newfoundland | 0.09 | 0.08 |
| Prince Edward Island | 0.27 | 0.07 | Prince Edward Island | 0.22 | 0.04 |
| Nova Scotia | 0.23 | 0.02 | Nova Scotia | 0.22 | 0.00 |
| New Brunswick | 0.22 | 0.03 | New Brunswick | 0.17 | -0.01 |
| Quebec | 0.17 | 0.08 | Quebec | 0.10 | 0.01 |
| Ontario | 0.27 | 0.02 | Ontario | 0.21 | 0.01 |
| Manitoba | 0.27 | 0.03 | Manitoba | 0.19 | -0.02 |
| Saskatchewan | 0.18 | -0.01 | Saskatchewan | 0.13 | -0.03 |
| Alberta | 0.33 | 0.04 | Alberta | 0.29 | 0.04 |
| British Columbia | 0.21 | 0.05 | British Columbia | 0.17 | 0.00 |
| **B. MATHEMATICS** | | | | | |
| **CANADA** | **0.16** | **0.01** | | | |
| France | 0.30 | 0.06 | | | |
| United States | 0.29 | 0.12 | | | |
| United Kingdom | 0.27 | 0.07 | | | |
| Germany | 0.06 | 0.08 | | | |
| Japan | 0.26 | 0.11 | | | |
| Italy | 0.25 | -0.03 | | | |
| Russian Federation | 0.24 | 0.12 | | | |
| Australia | 0.30 | 0.01 | | | |
| Belgium | 0.25 | 0.07 | | | |
| Finland | 0.12 | -0.01 | | | |
| Mexico | 0.14 | 0.21 | | | |
| Sweden | 0.01 | 0.01 | | | |
| Switzerland | -0.04 | 0.11 | | | |
| Newfoundland | 0.08 | 0.06 | | | |
| Prince Edward Island | 0.19 | 0.05 | | | |
| Nova Scotia | 0.17 | 0.02 | | | |
| New Brunswick | 0.14 | 0.04 | | | |
| Quebec | 0.12 | 0.04 | | | |
| Ontario | 0.21 | -0.02 | | | |
| Manitoba | 0.22 | 0.01 | | | |
| Saskatchewan | 0.11 | -0.02 | | | |
| Alberta | 0.29 | 0.01 | | | |
| British Columbia | 0.17 | 0.04 | | | |

## TABLE 2.5

### Effects of Student Career Expectations on Achievement Scores in Reading, Mathematics and Science

| Country and province | Standardized Effect | | | Country and province | Standardized Effect | | |
|---|---|---|---|---|---|---|---|
| | Reading | Mathematics | Science | | Reading | Mathematics | Science |
| **CANADA** | **0.23** | **0.18** | **0.20** | Sweden | 0.34 | 0.32 | 0.35 |
| | | | | Switzerland | 0.36 | 0.31 | 0.33 |
| France | 0.45 | 0.39 | 0.42 | Newfoundland | 0.24 | 0.21 | 0.22 |
| United States | 0.18 | 0.12 | 0.17 | Prince Edward Island | 0.22 | 0.15 | 0.20 |
| United Kingdom | 0.32 | 0.29 | 0.30 | Nova Scotia | 0.21 | 0.21 | 0.18 |
| Germany | 0.40 | 0.34 | 0.35 | New Brunswick | 0.25 | 0.18 | 0.21 |
| Japan | 0.21 | 0.21 | 0.21 | Quebec | 0.22 | 0.18 | 0.19 |
| Italy | 0.26 | 0.18 | 0.24 | Ontario | 0.23 | 0.20 | 0.20 |
| Russian Federation | 0.40 | 0.33 | 0.33 | Manitoba | 0.24 | 0.19 | 0.22 |
| Australia | 0.30 | 0.35 | 0.30 | Saskatchewan | 0.30 | 0.21 | 0.28 |
| Belgium | 0.46 | 0.43 | 0.42 | Alberta | 0.22 | 0.16 | 0.21 |
| Finland | 0.28 | 0.29 | 0.30 | British Columbia | 0.24 | 0.21 | 0.22 |
| Mexico | 0.13 | 0.14 | 0.12 | | | | |

## TABLE 2.6

### Average Achievement Scores in Reading, Mathematics and Science by Student Expectations of the Highest Level of Education

| Province | High school | Standard error | Trade school | Standard error | College | Standard error | One university degree | Standard error | More than one university degree | Standard error |
|---|---|---|---|---|---|---|---|---|---|---|
| **A. READING** | | | | | | | | | | |
| Newfoundland | 425 | (8.1) | 452 | (6.5) | 494 | (6.9) | 523 | (5.5) | 557 | (3.5) |
| Prince Edward Island | 451 | (7.5) | 486 | (13.6) | 475 | (8.1) | 527 | (5.0) | 548 | (3.4) |
| Nova Scotia | 441 | (8.8) | 475 | (6.8) | 492 | (6.9) | 532 | (3.8) | 550 | (3.1) |
| New Brunswick | 427 | (6.8) | 458 | (7.3) | 475 | (5.0) | 518 | (3.2) | 539 | (2.7) |
| Quebec | 439 | (6.5) | 489 | (4.9) | 531 | (3.2) | 569 | (3.2) | 565 | (4.7) |
| Ontario | 443 | (8.2) | 473 | (11.0) | 493 | (4.1) | 551 | (3.5) | 567 | (3.1) |
| Manitoba | 466 | (5.8) | 495 | (6.4) | 513 | (6.9) | 541 | (5.0) | 564 | (4.9) |
| Saskatchewan | 467 | (5.8) | 486 | (6.5) | 509 | (6.1) | 545 | (4.2) | 562 | (3.9) |
| Alberta | 477 | (7.4) | 491 | (7.3) | 525 | (4.4) | 562 | (4.6) | 589 | (4.2) |
| British Columbia | 471 | (8.3) | 488 | (8.3) | 507 | (4.9) | 547 | (3.7) | 573 | (3.1) |
| **B. MATHEMATICS** | | | | | | | | | | |
| Newfoundland | 445 | (9.8) | 478 | (7.0) | 490 | (9.1) | 511 | (5.8) | 536 | (4.0) |
| Prince Edward Island | 452 | (10.2) | s | s | 484 | (12.9) | 519 | (6.2) | 537 | (5.5) |
| Nova Scotia | 447 | (10.0) | 487 | (9.0) | 483 | (8.5) | 524 | (5.3) | 537 | (3.8) |
| New Brunswick | 443 | (8.4) | 490 | (10.0) | 488 | (5.9) | 523 | (4.1) | 527 | (3.7) |
| Quebec | 474 | (9.5) | 511 | (6.2) | 546 | (3.3) | 576 | (3.3) | 575 | (4.9) |
| Ontario | 463 | (8.5) | 485 | (9.5) | 491 | (4.5) | 538 | (3.9) | 549 | (3.6) |
| Manitoba | 482 | (8.9) | 515 | (9.5) | 524 | (8.8) | 543 | (5.0) | 559 | (5.0) |
| Saskatchewan | 477 | (6.4) | 506 | (7.8) | 505 | (9.0) | 539 | (4.6) | 549 | (5.0) |
| Alberta | 495 | (8.4) | 507 | (8.8) | 521 | (5.5) | 560 | (4.5) | 578 | (4.6) |
| British Columbia | 479 | (9.0) | 507 | (8.8) | 503 | (5.9) | 543 | (4.3) | 561 | (3.4) |

## TABLE 2.6 (continued)

### Average Achievement Scores in Reading, Mathematics and Science by Student Expectations of the Highest Level of Education

| Province | High school | Standard error | Trade school | Standard error | College | Standard error | One university degree | Standard error | More than one university degree | Standard error |
|---|---|---|---|---|---|---|---|---|---|---|
| | | | | | **C. SCIENCE** | | | | | |
| Newfoundland | 444 | (12.5) | 467 | (7.6) | 500 | (10.2) | 520 | (7.1) | 547 | (4.0) |
| Prince Edward Island | 454 | (9.0) | 475 | (17.5) | 483 | (12.0) | 516 | (5.0) | 533 | (4.2) |
| Nova Scotia | 445 | (10.3) | 484 | (10.1) | 492 | (7.9) | 530 | (4.9) | 540 | (4.7) |
| New Brunswick | 439 | (7.8) | 467 | (9.7) | 477 | (7.0) | 513 | (3.7) | 525 | (4.0) |
| Quebec | 457 | (8.8) | 503 | (5.7) | 537 | (5.0) | 569 | (4.4) | 563 | (6.0) |
| Ontario | 448 | (9.6) | 485 | (15.9) | 490 | (5.1) | 534 | (4.7) | 551 | (3.5) |
| Manitoba | 473 | (7.4) | 512 | (12.0) | 507 | (8.6) | 539 | (6.0) | 553 | (4.4) |
| Saskatchewan | 467 | (7.2) | 498 | (8.0) | 511 | (8.0) | 539 | (5.8) | 545 | (5.0) |
| Alberta | 481 | (9.5) | 505 | (11.5) | 519 | (5.6) | 556 | (5.9) | 580 | (4.3) |
| British Columbia | 479 | (9.7) | 502 | (12.4) | 508 | (5.7) | 535 | (4.6) | 563 | (4.0) |

## TABLE 2.7

### Average Achievement Scores in Reading, Mathematics and Science by School Year Job Status

| Province | With a job in the school year | Standard error | Without a job in the school year | Standard error | Province | With a job in the school year | Standard error | Without a job in the school year | Standard error |
|---|---|---|---|---|---|---|---|---|---|
| **A. READING** | | | | | **C. SCIENCE** | | | | |
| Newfoundland | **498** | (4.6) | **530** | (3.5) | Newfoundland | **503** | (6.0) | **525** | (4.4) |
| Prince Edward Island | **506** | (5.4) | **525** | (3.1) | Prince Edward Island | 502 | (6.4) | 513 | (3.5) |
| Nova Scotia | **505** | (4.7) | **530** | (2.9) | Nova Scotia | 504 | (6.9) | 522 | (3.6) |
| New Brunswick | **485** | (3.9) | **515** | (1.8) | New Brunswick | **487** | (4.9) | **506** | (2.6) |
| Quebec | **525** | (4.4) | **547** | (2.9) | Quebec | **532** | (4.9) | **549** | (3.3) |
| Ontario | **521** | (4.9) | **544** | (3.3) | Ontario | 519 | (5.8) | 528 | (3.8) |
| Manitoba | **511** | (6.3) | **541** | (3.4) | Manitoba | 517 | (6.7) | 534 | (3.6) |
| Saskatchewan | **511** | (5.0) | **538** | (3.1) | Saskatchewan | **503** | (7.1) | **529** | (3.3) |
| Alberta | **537** | (5.3) | **560** | (3.3) | Alberta | 543 | (6.0) | 553 | (3.8) |
| British Columbia | **517** | (4.5) | **552** | (3.2) | British Columbia | **517** | (6.0) | **543** | (3.8) |

Note: Average scores are bolded for jurisdictions where there are significant differences between girls and boys.

**B. MATHEMATICS**

| Province | With a job in the school year | Standard error | Without a job in the school year | Standard error |
|---|---|---|---|---|
| Newfoundland | 500 | (5.2) | 516 | (3.6) |
| Prince Edward Island | 509 | (6.5) | 517 | (4.4) |
| Nova Scotia | **501** | (5.4) | **519** | (3.5) |
| New Brunswick | 502 | (4.4) | 514 | (2.6) |
| Quebec | 545 | (4.4) | 558 | (3.0) |
| Ontario | **514** | (5.2) | **531** | (2.9) |
| Manitoba | **518** | (8.0) | **543** | (3.7) |
| Saskatchewan | **510** | (5.7) | **532** | (3.2) |
| Alberta | 541 | (6.4) | 553 | (3.2) |
| British Columbia | **522** | (4.9) | **542** | (3.4) |

## TABLE 2.8

**Effects of Weekday and Weekend Work Hours During the School Year on Achievement Scores in Reading, Mathematics and Science**

| Province | Standardized Effect | | Province | Standardized Effect | |
|---|---|---|---|---|---|
| | Weekday work hours | Weekend work hours | | Weekday work hours | Weekend work hours |
| **A. READING** | | | **C. SCIENCE** | | |
| Newfoundland | -0.21 | -0.22 | Newfoundland | -0.16 | -0.18 |
| Prince Edward Island | -0.25 | -0.21 | Prince Edward Island | -0.22 | -0.19 |
| Nova Scotia | -0.23 | -0.20 | Nova Scotia | -0.22 | -0.19 |
| New Brunswick | -0.29 | -0.29 | New Brunswick | -0.27 | -0.23 |
| Quebec | -0.26 | -0.21 | Quebec | -0.24 | -0.19 |
| Ontario | -0.25 | -0.22 | Ontario | -0.25 | -0.16 |
| Manitoba | -0.29 | -0.25 | Manitoba | -0.28 | -0.21 |
| Saskatchewan | -0.27 | -0.26 | Saskatchewan | -0.21 | -0.23 |
| Alberta | -0.24 | -0.21 | Alberta | -0.24 | -0.18 |
| British Columbia | -0.23 | -0.24 | British Columbia | -0.19 | -0.21 |
| **B. MATHEMATICS** | | | | | |
| Newfoundland | -0.20 | -0.16 | | | |
| Prince Edward Island | -0.22 | -0.18 | | | |
| Nova Scotia | -0.17 | -0.17 | | | |
| New Brunswick | -0.23 | -0.21 | | | |
| Quebec | -0.21 | -0.16 | | | |
| Ontario | -0.21 | -0.20 | | | |
| Manitoba | -0.21 | -0.22 | | | |
| Saskatchewan | -0.17 | -0.21 | | | |
| Alberta | -0.23 | -0.17 | | | |
| British Columbia | -0.23 | -0.18 | | | |

## TABLE 2.9

### The Relative Impact of Individual Factors on Achievement Scores in Reading, Mathematics and Science

| | CANADA | France | United States | United Kingdom | Germany | Japan | Italy | Russian Federation | Australia | Belgium | Finland | Mexico | Sweden | Switzerland | Newfoundland | Prince Edward Island | Nova Scotia | New Brunswick | Quebec | Ontario | Manitoba | Saskatchewan | Alberta | British Columbia |
|---|---|---|---|---|---|---|---|---|---|---|---|---|---|---|---|---|---|---|---|---|---|---|---|---|
| **A. READING** | | | | | | | | | | | | | | | | | | | | | | | | |
| Reading enjoyment | m | s | m | m | m | s | s | s | m | s | m | | m | m | m | m | m | m | m | m | m | m | m | m |
| Time spent in reading | | | | | -s | | | | | | | | | | | | | | | | | | | |
| Reading diversity | | s | | | s | s | s | | s | s | s | s | s | s | | | s | s | | | | | | |
| Use of public and school library | -s | -s | | -s | | | -s | -s | | | -s | | | -s | | | | | -s | -s | | | | -s |
| Homework time | | s | s | s | | s | s | s | | | | | -s | | | | | | | s | | | s | |
| Sense of belonging to school | | | | | | | | | | | | | s | | | | | | | | | | | |
| Girls versus boys | | | | | | | | s | | s | s | | | | | | | | | | | | | |
| Student career expectations | s | m | s | m | m | s | s | s | m | s | s | s | m | s | s | s | s | s | s | s | s | s | s | s |
| **B. MATHEMATICS** | | | | | | | | | | | | | | | | | | | | | | | | |
| Reading enjoyment | s | | s | s | m | | s | s | s | s | s | | s | s | s | s | m | s | s | s | m | m | m | s |
| Time spent in reading | | | | -s | -s | | | | | -s | -s | | | | | | | | | | | | | |
| Reading diversity | | s | s | | s | s | s | | | s | s | s | s | s | | | s | s | s | | | | | |
| Use of public and school library | | -s | | -s | | | -s | -s | | | -s | | | | -s | | -s | | -s | -s | | | | -s |
| Homework time | | s | s | s | | s | s | s | s | | | | s | -s | | | s | | | | | | s | |
| Sense of belonging of school | | | | | | | | | | | | | | | | | | | | | | | | |
| Girls versus boys | -s | -s | -s | -s | -s | -s | -s | -s | | -s | -s | | -s | -s | -s | -s | -s | -s | -s | -s | -s | -s | -s | -s |
| Student career expectations | s | m | s | s | m | s | s | s | m | m | s | s | s | m | s | s | s | s | s | s | s | s | s | s |
| **C. SCIENCE** | | | | | | | | | | | | | | | | | | | | | | | | |
| Reading enjoyment | m | s | m | m | m | s | s | s | s | s | m | | m | s | m | m | m | m | m | m | m | m | m | m |
| Time spent in reading | | | -s | | -s | | | | | | | | | | | | | | | | | | | |
| Reading diversity | | s | s | | s | s | | | s | s | s | s | s | | | | s | | | | | | | |
| Use of public and school library | | | -s | | | | -s | -s | | | -s | -s | | | -s | | | | | -s | | | | -s |
| Homework time | | s | s | s | | s | s | s | s | | | | -s | | | | | | | | | | s | |
| Sense of belonging to school | | | | | | | | | | | | | | | | | | | | | | | | |
| Girls versus boys | -s | -s | -s | -s | -s | | | | | -s | | | -s | -s | -s | -s | -s | | -s | -s | -s | -s | -s | -s |
| Student career expectations | s | m | s | s | m | | s | s | m | m | s | s | s | m | s | s | s | s | s | s | s | s | s | s |

Note:   In each domain, a multiple regression analysis was performed for each country and province. Significant effects are identified as small (s), moderate (m) or large (l), using the criteria outlined in the chapter. Variables with a negative effect are indicated with a "-" sign. Variables with trivial effect sizes, less than |0.10|, are not shown.

## TABLE 3.1

### Average Achievement Scores in Reading, Mathematics and Science by Family Structure

| Country and province | Single-parent family | Standard error | Two-parent family | Standard error | Country and province | Single-parent family | Standard error | Two-parent family | Standard error |
|---|---|---|---|---|---|---|---|---|---|
| **A. READING** | | | | | **C. SCIENCE** | | | | |
| **CANADA** | 527 | (2.5) | 538 | (1.5) | **CANADA** | 520 | (2.2) | 533 | (1.5) |
| France | **488** | (4.7) | **509** | (2.7) | France | **487** | (5.0) | **505** | (3.2) |
| United States | **484** | (8.6) | **524** | (6.2) | United States | **477** | (9.4) | **517** | (7.0) |
| United Kingdom | **502** | (3.2) | **533** | (2.9) | United Kingdom | **512** | (4.5) | **541** | (2.9) |
| Germany | 478 | (5.4) | 488 | (2.6) | Germany | 483 | (5.6) | 491 | (2.7) |
| Japan | 510 | (8.6) | 527 | (5.1) | Japan | 534 | (10.6) | 555 | (5.3) |
| Italy | 481 | (4.5) | 492 | (2.6) | Italy | 474 | (5.9) | 481 | (3.0) |
| Russian Federation | 462 | (4.8) | 464 | (4.1) | Russian Federation | 454 | (6.3) | 463 | (4.9) |
| Australia | 521 | (4.7) | 532 | (3.9) | Australia | 523 | (5.5) | 530 | (3.8) |
| Belgium | **487** | (5.5) | **513** | (3.7) | Belgium | **475** | (7.1) | **502** | (4.4) |
| Finland | **529** | (6.8) | **553** | (2.2) | Finland | **521** | (5.1) | **543** | (2.5) |
| Mexico | 419 | (4.4) | 424 | (3.7) | Mexico | 427 | (5.1) | 421 | (3.5) |
| Sweden | **501** | (4.0) | **522** | (2.0) | Sweden | **495** | (5.4) | **518** | (2.3) |
| Switzerland | 496 | (6.0) | 497 | (4.3) | Switzerland | 495 | (8.0) | 498 | (4.5) |
| Newfoundland | 519 | (7.8) | 519 | (2.9) | Newfoundland | 518 | (9.6) | 518 | (4.0) |
| Prince Edward Island | 508 | (6.2) | 521 | (2.6) | Prince Edward Island | 503 | (8.0) | 510 | (2.9) |
| Nova Scotia | 514 | (7.4) | 525 | (2.2) | Nova Scotia | 513 | (10.0) | 518 | (3.3) |
| New Brunswick | **487** | (5.0) | **507** | (2.0) | New Brunswick | **482** | (6.3) | **502** | (2.5) |
| Quebec | 530 | (5.8) | 539 | (2.9) | Quebec | 538 | (8.2) | 543 | (3.4) |
| Ontario | 528 | (4.6) | 537 | (3.2) | Ontario | 511 | (5.3) | 526 | (3.3) |
| Manitoba | **512** | (6.7) | **535** | (3.4) | Manitoba | **506** | (9.0) | **533** | (3.4) |
| Saskatchewan | **515** | (5.6) | **533** | (2.9) | Saskatchewan | 509 | (7.5) | 526 | (3.2) |
| Alberta | **537** | (5.3) | **555** | (3.4) | Alberta | **531** | (6.5) | **552** | (3.5) |
| British Columbia | **527** | (4.7) | **543** | (3.2) | British Columbia | 520 | (5.4) | 538 | (3.6) |

Note: Where differences in average achievement between those from single-parent and two-parent families are significant, scores are bolded.

### B. MATHEMATICS

| Country and province | Single-parent family | Standard error | Two-parent family | Standard error |
|---|---|---|---|---|
| **CANADA** | 520 | (2.2) | 537 | (1.5) |
| France | **499** | (5.7) | **522** | (2.8) |
| United States | **470** | (9.5) | **514** | (7.0) |
| United Kingdom | **510** | (3.8) | **538** | (2.8) |
| Germany | 479 | (5.9) | 494 | (2.6) |
| Japan | 543 | (9.4) | 561 | (5.4) |
| Italy | 448 | (4.7) | 462 | (2.8) |
| Russian Federation | 472 | (5.8) | 483 | (5.5) |
| Australia | 524 | (5.7) | 536 | (3.7) |
| Belgium | **501** | (6.9) | **525** | (3.9) |
| Finland | **522** | (5.1) | **541** | (2.1) |
| Mexico | 379 | (5.3) | 391 | (3.6) |
| Sweden | **493** | (5.1) | **516** | (2.7) |
| Switzerland | 525 | (6.4) | 533 | (4.5) |
| Newfoundland | 501 | (8.3) | 512 | (3.1) |
| Prince Edward Island | 501 | (7.6) | 516 | (4.0) |
| Nova Scotia | 507 | (7.9) | 517 | (2.7) |
| New Brunswick | **493** | (5.5) | **511** | (2.5) |
| Quebec | **534** | (6.0) | **555** | (2.8) |
| Ontario | 515 | (4.8) | 527 | (3.1) |
| Manitoba | **508** | (7.7) | **540** | (3.6) |
| Saskatchewan | **510** | (6.4) | **529** | (3.1) |
| Alberta | **524** | (5.8) | **553** | (3.7) |
| British Columbia | 523 | (4.8) | 538 | (3.2) |

## TABLE 3.2

### Effects of Number of Siblings on Achievement Scores in Reading, Mathematics and Science

| Country and province | Standardized Effect | | |
|---|---|---|---|
| | Reading | Mathematics | Science |
| **CANADA** | **-0.09** | **-0.10** | **-0.11** |
| France | -0.18 | -0.16 | -0.19 |
| United States | -0.23 | -0.23 | -0.24 |
| United Kingdom | -0.18 | -0.20 | -0.20 |
| Germany | -0.17 | -0.15 | -0.17 |
| Japan | -0.04 | -0.02 | -0.04 |
| Italy | -0.18 | -0.16 | -0.20 |
| Russian Federation | -0.16 | -0.12 | -0.11 |
| Australia | -0.11 | -0.12 | -0.09 |
| Belgium | -0.23 | -0.22 | -0.22 |
| Finland | -0.07 | -0.05 | -0.03 |
| Mexico | -0.31 | -0.30 | -0.26 |
| Sweden | -0.13 | -0.12 | -0.13 |
| Switzerland | -0.10 | -0.04 | -0.06 |
| Newfoundland | -0.06 | -0.05 | -0.10 |
| Prince Edward Island | -0.04 | -0.04 | -0.03 |
| Nova Scotia | -0.06 | -0.07 | -0.06 |
| New Brunswick | -0.06 | -0.07 | -0.07 |
| Quebec | -0.09 | -0.10 | -0.11 |
| Ontario | -0.09 | -0.08 | -0.10 |
| Manitoba | -0.13 | -0.10 | -0.15 |
| Saskatchewan | -0.10 | -0.13 | -0.11 |
| Alberta | -0.12 | -0.12 | -0.11 |
| British Columbia | -0.09 | -0.11 | -0.12 |

## TABLE 3.3

### Effects of Family Socio-economic Status on Achievement Scores in Reading, Mathematics and Science

| Country and province | Standardized Effect | | |
|---|---|---|---|
| | Reading | Mathematics | Science |
| **CANADA** | **0.27** | **0.25** | **0.26** |
| France | 0.36 | 0.32 | 0.35 |
| United States | 0.34 | 0.38 | 0.35 |
| United Kingdom | 0.38 | 0.38 | 0.38 |
| Germany | 0.40 | 0.38 | 0.38 |
| Japan | 0.08 | 0.12 | 0.09 |
| Italy | 0.28 | 0.23 | 0.25 |
| Russian Federation | 0.30 | 0.24 | 0.26 |
| Australia | 0.33 | 0.34 | 0.28 |
| Belgium | 0.37 | 0.38 | 0.38 |
| Finland | 0.23 | 0.24 | 0.21 |
| Mexico | 0.39 | 0.37 | 0.35 |
| Sweden | 0.30 | 0.33 | 0.27 |
| Switzerland | 0.40 | 0.35 | 0.41 |
| Newfoundland | 0.34 | 0.28 | 0.34 |
| Prince Edward Island | 0.27 | 0.23 | 0.25 |
| Nova Scotia | 0.31 | 0.33 | 0.30 |
| New Brunswick | 0.27 | 0.22 | 0.27 |
| Quebec | 0.26 | 0.27 | 0.26 |
| Ontario | 0.29 | 0.28 | 0.27 |
| Manitoba | 0.23 | 0.21 | 0.23 |
| Saskatchewan | 0.16 | 0.14 | 0.13 |
| Alberta | 0.27 | 0.25 | 0.28 |
| British Columbia | 0.25 | 0.22 | 0.26 |

## TABLE 3.4

### Average Scores in Reading, Mathematics and Science, within National and Provincial Quarters of Family Socio-economic Status

| Country and province | First quarter average | Standard error | Second quarter average | Standard error | Third quarter average | Standard error | Fourth quarter average | Standard error | Difference between fourth quarter and first quarter |
|---|---|---|---|---|---|---|---|---|---|
| **A. READING** | | | | | | | | | |
| **CANADA** | 503 | (2.2) | 528 | (2.1) | 542 | (1.9) | 568 | (2.0) | 65 |
| France | 468 | (4.6) | 493 | (3.3) | 520 | (3.1) | 552 | (3.5) | 84 |
| United States | 466 | (7.1) | 503 | (6.7) | 525 | (6.0) | 554 | (6.1) | 89 |
| United Kingdom | 481 | (3.1) | 512 | (3.7) | 535 | (3.3) | 578 | (3.4) | 97 |
| Germany | 424 | (5.6) | 469 | (4.0) | 511 | (3.3) | 540 | (3.5) | 116 |
| Japan | 531 | (8.1) | 520 | (7.3) | 551 | (6.3) | 547 | (6.9) | 17 |
| Italy | 457 | (4.3) | 480 | (3.3) | 493 | (3.7) | 525 | (3.8) | 67 |
| Russian Federation | 428 | (5.7) | 450 | (3.8) | 472 | (4.7) | 502 | (3.8) | 74 |
| Australia | 490 | (3.8) | 522 | (4.6) | 537 | (4.2) | 575 | (5.3) | 85 |
| Belgium | 459 | (6.4) | 489 | (4.4) | 536 | (3.1) | 560 | (3.4) | 101 |
| Finland | 522 | (4.8) | 535 | (3.2) | 555 | (3.1) | 577 | (3.3) | 54 |
| Mexico | 385 | (4.5) | 403 | (3.5) | 434 | (4.0) | 470 | (5.8) | 86 |
| Sweden | 484 | (3.0) | 506 | (3.1) | 523 | (3.2) | 557 | (3.2) | 72 |
| Switzerland | 432 | (4.3) | 492 | (4.7) | 513 | (4.4) | 549 | (5.3) | 117 |
| Newfoundland | 478 | (4.2) | 508 | (4.7) | 528 | (5.5) | 563 | (4.9) | 85 |
| Prince Edward Island | 484 | (4.2) | 513 | (5.7) | 521 | (4.2) | 557 | (4.6) | 72 |
| Nova Scotia | 485 | (4.4) | 520 | (4.7) | 530 | (3.8) | 558 | (4.4) | 73 |
| New Brunswick | 467 | (4.3) | 494 | (3.6) | 511 | (3.8) | 539 | (4.0) | 72 |
| Quebec | 508 | (3.8) | 532 | (4.0) | 546 | (3.5) | 567 | (3.7) | 60 |
| Ontario | 498 | (5.4) | 525 | (3.4) | 547 | (4.2) | 571 | (4.2) | 74 |
| Manitoba | 501 | (4.8) | 525 | (5.4) | 540 | (4.8) | 558 | (5.5) | 56 |
| Saskatchewan | 510 | (4.8) | 530 | (3.9) | 528 | (4.8) | 551 | (4.1) | 40 |
| Alberta | 515 | (4.9) | 548 | (4.7) | 554 | (4.2) | 587 | (4.9) | 72 |
| British Columbia | 510 | (4.6) | 533 | (4.0) | 546 | (3.8) | 568 | (3.7) | 58 |
| **B. MATHEMATICS** | | | | | | | | | |
| **CANADA** | 508 | (2.1) | 527 | (2.3) | 539 | (2.1) | 563 | (2.3) | 55 |
| France | 486 | (5.0) | 507 | (4.0) | 530 | (3.5) | 560 | (3.8) | 74 |
| United States | 453 | (7.5) | 491 | (8.9) | 510 | (7.1) | 548 | (6.5) | 95 |
| United Kingdom | 488 | (3.3) | 523 | (4.2) | 542 | (3.7) | 576 | (3.8) | 88 |
| Germany | 434 | (5.5) | 480 | (5.6) | 513 | (3.6) | 540 | (4.2) | 106 |
| Japan | 559 | (9.7) | 559 | (7.9) | 582 | (7.9) | 586 | (9.6) | 27 |
| Italy | 433 | (5.1) | 442 | (5.2) | 465 | (3.8) | 486 | (4.9) | 54 |
| Russian Federation | 450 | (7.5) | 466 | (6.3) | 487 | (6.7) | 515 | (5.1) | 64 |
| Australia | 493 | (4.4) | 527 | (4.6) | 542 | (5.1) | 577 | (5.7) | 84 |
| Belgium | 474 | (7.3) | 499 | (4.9) | 547 | (3.9) | 575 | (4.2) | 101 |
| Finland | 512 | (3.6) | 528 | (3.4) | 542 | (3.1) | 564 | (3.7) | 52 |
| Mexico | 352 | (5.4) | 372 | (3.9) | 396 | (5.0) | 432 | (5.9) | 80 |
| Sweden | 474 | (4.3) | 499 | (4.5) | 517 | (3.8) | 554 | (4.0) | 80 |
| Switzerland | 475 | (4.7) | 533 | (5.0) | 539 | (5.9) | 578 | (5.2) | 104 |
| Newfoundland | 478 | (4.8) | 504 | (4.6) | 528 | (5.7) | 535 | (6.1) | 57 |
| Prince Edward Island | 490 | (5.9) | 506 | (6.2) | 516 | (5.4) | 542 | (6.1) | 52 |
| Nova Scotia | 472 | (5.2) | 518 | (5.0) | 517 | (5.4) | 549 | (4.8) | 77 |
| New Brunswick | 487 | (4.8) | 502 | (3.7) | 508 | (4.7) | 534 | (5.0) | 47 |
| Quebec | 524 | (4.7) | 545 | (4.1) | 559 | (4.0) | 580 | (3.7) | 56 |
| Ontario | 497 | (4.8) | 510 | (4.2) | 533 | (4.9) | 558 | (4.6) | 61 |
| Manitoba | 510 | (6.4) | 531 | (6.6) | 543 | (5.6) | 554 | (5.8) | 44 |
| Saskatchewan | 506 | (4.9) | 531 | (4.9) | 528 | (4.9) | 540 | (5.1) | 34 |
| Alberta | 521 | (4.9) | 540 | (6.0) | 550 | (4.4) | 579 | (5.5) | 57 |
| British Columbia | 511 | (5.4) | 534 | (4.7) | 537 | (4.5) | 560 | (4.3) | 49 |

**TABLE 3.4 (Continued)**

## Average Scores in Reading, Mathematics and Science, within National and Provincial Quarters of Family Socio-economic Status

| Country and province | First quarter average | Standard error | Second quarter average | Standard error | Third quarter average | Standard error | Fourth quarter average | Standard error | Difference between fourth quarter and first quarter |
|---|---|---|---|---|---|---|---|---|---|
| **C. SCIENCE** | | | | | | | | | |
| **CANADA** | **501** | **(2.7)** | **523** | **(2.5)** | **537** | **(1.8)** | **560** | **(2.3)** | **59** |
| France | 463 | (5.0) | 481 | (4.9) | 518 | (4.5) | 555 | (4.5) | 93 |
| United States | 463 | (8.2) | 492 | (6.5) | 518 | (6.6) | 555 | (7.8) | 91 |
| United Kingdom | 492 | (4.1) | 520 | (3.6) | 542 | (4.0) | 588 | (3.8) | 96 |
| Germany | 434 | (5.4) | 471 | (5.4) | 511 | (3.9) | 538 | (3.8) | 104 |
| Japan | 554 | (9.8) | 545 | (8.3) | 575 | (7.3) | 575 | (8.4) | 21 |
| Italy | 452 | (5.1) | 469 | (4.6) | 482 | (5.1) | 514 | (4.2) | 62 |
| Russian Federation | 431 | (5.8) | 447 | (5.5) | 469 | (5.2) | 499 | (5.6) | 68 |
| Australia | 497 | (4.9) | 521 | (4.7) | 531 | (4.5) | 570 | (5.9) | 73 |
| Belgium | 446 | (8.8) | 479 | (4.9) | 522 | (3.6) | 552 | (4.1) | 106 |
| Finland | 518 | (4.6) | 524 | (3.7) | 544 | (4.1) | 565 | (4.4) | 47 |
| Mexico | 393 | (4.6) | 406 | (3.8) | 429 | (4.5) | 461 | (6.3) | 68 |
| Sweden | 484 | (3.7) | 498 | (4.1) | 519 | (4.0) | 552 | (3.8) | 68 |
| Switzerland | 439 | (4.9) | 486 | (5.7) | 510 | (5.0) | 554 | (5.9) | 114 |
| Newfoundland | 482 | (5.9) | 507 | (4.7) | 524 | (7.4) | 560 | (5.9) | 78 |
| Prince Edward Island | 482 | (5.6) | 505 | (6.2) | 506 | (5.7) | 542 | (5.2) | 60 |
| Nova Scotia | 482 | (5.2) | 513 | (6.3) | 525 | (5.4) | 549 | (5.9) | 67 |
| New Brunswick | 465 | (4.8) | 492 | (4.1) | 503 | (4.7) | 532 | (5.1) | 66 |
| Quebec | 513 | (4.8) | 535 | (5.0) | 550 | (4.7) | 573 | (5.1) | 61 |
| Ontario | 493 | (6.5) | 511 | (4.9) | 532 | (3.9) | 554 | (5.0) | 62 |
| Manitoba | 500 | (5.5) | 528 | (7.4) | 532 | (5.8) | 554 | (5.5) | 54 |
| Saskatchewan | 509 | (5.1) | 524 | (5.1) | 518 | (5.9) | 538 | (4.9) | 29 |
| Alberta | 514 | (5.5) | 540 | (5.0) | 549 | (4.8) | 585 | (5.9) | 71 |
| British Columbia | 505 | (5.7) | 528 | (5.1) | 540 | (4.3) | 560 | (4.6) | 54 |

## TABLE 3.5

### Effects of Family Possessions, Home Educational Resources, Home Cultural Possessions and Students' Cultural Activities on Achievement Scores in Reading, Mathematics and Science

| Country and province | Family posses-sions | Home educa-tional resources | Home cultural posses-sions | Student's cultural activities | Country and province | Family posses-sions | Home educa-tional resources | Home cultural posses-sions | Student's cultural activities |
|---|---|---|---|---|---|---|---|---|---|
| **A. READING** | | | | | **C. SCIENCE** | | | | |
| **CANADA** | **0.13** | **0.18** | **0.24** | **0.26** | **CANADA** | **0.12** | **0.15** | **0.20** | **0.22** |
| France | 0.22 | 0.28 | 0.35 | 0.27 | France | 0.19 | 0.24 | 0.30 | 0.26 |
| United States | 0.29 | 0.33 | 0.32 | 0.27 | United States | 0.28 | 0.32 | 0.32 | 0.27 |
| United Kingdom | 0.13 | 0.25 | 0.31 | 0.30 | United Kingdom | 0.16 | 0.26 | 0.29 | 0.28 |
| Germany | 0.20 | 0.28 | 0.30 | 0.30 | Germany | 0.18 | 0.24 | 0.27 | 0.28 |
| Japan | 0.03 | 0.20 | 0.23 | 0.20 | Japan | 0.00 | 0.17 | 0.21 | 0.20 |
| Italy | 0.09 | 0.16 | 0.23 | 0.20 | Italy | 0.11 | 0.18 | 0.19 | 0.18 |
| Russian Federation | 0.12 | 0.24 | 0.20 | 0.19 | Russian Federation | 0.11 | 0.19 | 0.15 | 0.18 |
| Australia | 0.14 | 0.23 | 0.32 | 0.27 | Australia | 0.13 | 0.23 | 0.29 | 0.22 |
| Belgium | 0.07 | 0.33 | 0.30 | 0.34 | Belgium | 0.12 | 0.32 | 0.31 | 0.32 |
| Finland | 0.10 | 0.14 | 0.24 | 0.17 | Finland | 0.12 | 0.14 | 0.19 | 0.12 |
| Mexico | 0.33 | 0.37 | 0.32 | 0.31 | Mexico | 0.33 | 0.33 | 0.30 | 0.32 |
| Sweden | 0.07 | 0.15 | 0.28 | 0.16 | Sweden | 0.08 | 0.13 | 0.23 | 0.10 |
| Switzerland | 0.11 | 0.24 | 0.26 | 0.24 | Switzerland | 0.12 | 0.19 | 0.24 | 0.23 |
| Newfoundland | 0.17 | 0.19 | 0.27 | 0.31 | Newfoundland | 0.19 | 0.17 | 0.23 | 0.29 |
| Prince Edward Island | 0.08 | 0.15 | 0.25 | 0.30 | Prince Edward Island | 0.08 | 0.12 | 0.24 | 0.25 |
| Nova Scotia | 0.15 | 0.15 | 0.28 | 0.29 | Nova Scotia | 0.17 | 0.12 | 0.27 | 0.26 |
| New Brunswick | 0.14 | 0.17 | 0.28 | 0.24 | New Brunswick | 0.16 | 0.17 | 0.24 | 0.19 |
| Quebec | 0.12 | 0.17 | 0.21 | 0.25 | Quebec | 0.11 | 0.15 | 0.16 | 0.20 |
| Ontario | 0.14 | 0.18 | 0.26 | 0.27 | Ontario | 0.11 | 0.15 | 0.23 | 0.23 |
| Manitoba | 0.14 | 0.13 | 0.24 | 0.23 | Manitoba | 0.18 | 0.08 | 0.19 | 0.17 |
| Saskatchewan | 0.10 | 0.13 | 0.20 | 0.25 | Saskatchewan | 0.12 | 0.12 | 0.18 | 0.22 |
| Alberta | 0.12 | 0.21 | 0.28 | 0.27 | Alberta | 0.14 | 0.20 | 0.27 | 0.25 |
| British Columbia | 0.09 | 0.16 | 0.23 | 0.26 | British Columbia | 0.13 | 0.15 | 0.21 | 0.23 |
| **B. MATHEMATICS** | | | | | | | | | |
| **CANADA** | **0.13** | **0.16** | **0.16** | **0.19** | | | | | |
| France | 0.23 | 0.28 | 0.28 | 0.22 | | | | | |
| United States | 0.38 | 0.36 | 0.33 | 0.26 | | | | | |
| United Kingdom | 0.17 | 0.27 | 0.27 | 0.26 | | | | | |
| Germany | 0.22 | 0.28 | 0.28 | 0.26 | | | | | |
| Japan | 0.07 | 0.19 | 0.13 | 0.14 | | | | | |
| Italy | 0.12 | 0.16 | 0.17 | 0.14 | | | | | |
| Russian Federation | 0.12 | 0.24 | 0.17 | 0.13 | | | | | |
| Australia | 0.16 | 0.20 | 0.26 | 0.25 | | | | | |
| Belgium | 0.12 | 0.34 | 0.25 | 0.31 | | | | | |
| Finland | 0.15 | 0.18 | 0.18 | 0.11 | | | | | |
| Mexico | 0.33 | 0.35 | 0.33 | 0.29 | | | | | |
| Sweden | 0.13 | 0.19 | 0.26 | 0.11 | | | | | |
| Switzerland | 0.11 | 0.24 | 0.18 | 0.17 | | | | | |
| Newfoundland | 0.19 | 0.17 | 0.17 | 0.24 | | | | | |
| Prince Edward Island | 0.12 | 0.17 | 0.15 | 0.20 | | | | | |
| Nova Scotia | 0.21 | 0.19 | 0.23 | 0.20 | | | | | |
| New Brunswick | 0.15 | 0.15 | 0.15 | 0.15 | | | | | |
| Quebec | 0.17 | 0.18 | 0.16 | 0.20 | | | | | |
| Ontario | 0.15 | 0.14 | 0.20 | 0.21 | | | | | |
| Manitoba | 0.22 | 0.14 | 0.19 | 0.18 | | | | | |
| Saskatchewan | 0.15 | 0.12 | 0.12 | 0.16 | | | | | |
| Alberta | 0.15 | 0.21 | 0.21 | 0.19 | | | | | |
| British Columbia | 0.12 | 0.15 | 0.18 | 0.17 | | | | | |

## TABLE 3.6

### Average Achievement Scores in Reading, Mathematics and Science by Number of Books at Home

| Country and province | None | | 1–10 | | 11–50 | | 51–100 | | 101–250 | | 251–500 | | More than 500 | |
|---|---|---|---|---|---|---|---|---|---|---|---|---|---|---|
| **A. READING** | | | | | | | | | | | | | | |
| **CANADA** | **421** | **(10.5)** | **474** | **(3.7)** | **507** | **(2.8)** | **528** | **(2.0)** | **546** | **(2.0)** | **562** | **(2.1)** | **563** | **(2.7)** |
| France | 396 | (9.5) | 441 | (5.2) | 488 | (3.4) | 509 | (3.2) | 531 | (3.2) | 556 | (3.6) | 548 | (5.3) |
| United States | 377 | (10.8) | 431 | (7.8) | 480 | (6.8) | 507 | (5.3) | 535 | (6.5) | 559 | (7.3) | 560 | (8.3) |
| United Kingdom | 396 | (12.9) | 447 | (5.2) | 494 | (3.1) | 514 | (3.1) | 547 | (3.6) | 568 | (4.0) | 577 | (5.1) |
| Germany | 348 | (19.8) | 364 | (15.4) | 443 | (4.8) | 473 | (3.8) | 512 | (3.6) | 539 | (3.8) | 549 | (4.5) |
| Japan | 448 | (17.4) | 495 | (7.8) | 511 | (5.8) | 523 | (5.1) | 540 | (4.9) | 545 | (5.0) | 553 | (6.7) |
| Italy | 377 | (20.0) | 433 | (7.8) | 468 | (4.1) | 484 | (3.3) | 507 | (3.6) | 517 | (6.4) | 520 | (5.8) |
| Russian Federation | 360 | (15.6) | 398 | (5.0) | 427 | (5.5) | 447 | (5.0) | 481 | (3.7) | 494 | (4.7) | 496 | (4.8) |
| Australia | 456 | (16.1) | 449 | (9.6) | 489 | (4.5) | 517 | (4.0) | 538 | (5.1) | 555 | (4.6) | 562 | (6.4) |
| Belgium | 395 | (12.0) | 451 | (5.4) | 501 | (4.3) | 511 | (4.6) | 541 | (3.6) | 559 | (3.8) | 547 | (5.7) |
| Finland | 480 | (17.7) | 500 | (6.7) | 528 | (3.3) | 537 | (2.9) | 565 | (3.7) | 576 | (3.9) | 581 | (6.8) |
| Mexico | 357 | (6.7) | 391 | (3.1) | 420 | (3.3) | 446 | (3.7) | 468 | (6.1) | 497 | (9.2) | 469 | (11.9) |
| Sweden | 420 | (13.6) | 439 | (8.5) | 477 | (3.2) | 502 | (3.4) | 522 | (3.1) | 545 | (3.4) | 556 | (3.8) |
| Switzerland | 390 | (16.0) | 407 | (5.4) | 457 | (4.3) | 485 | (4.5) | 517 | (4.9) | 548 | (4.4) | 546 | (8.3) |
| Newfoundland | S | S | 436 | (10.1) | 489 | (5.2) | 505 | (5.8) | 526 | (5.2) | 538 | (6.2) | 552 | (7.6) |
| Prince Edward Island | S | S | 457 | (10.6) | 492 | (5.6) | 502 | (5.2) | 533 | (5.1) | 545 | (5.5) | 546 | (6.0) |
| Nova Scotia | S | S | 459 | (11.9) | 489 | (5.7) | 504 | (4.0) | 524 | (3.8) | 550 | (4.6) | 549 | (5.5) |
| New Brunswick | 387 | (16.4) | 432 | (5.8) | 478 | (3.6) | 494 | (3.4) | 517 | (3.6) | 532 | (5.0) | 535 | (5.2) |
| Quebec | 434 | (12.0) | 486 | (6.9) | 520 | (4.2) | 539 | (3.9) | 557 | (3.5) | 567 | (5.0) | 567 | (5.5) |
| Ontario | S | S | 468 | (8.1) | 496 | (5.9) | 526 | (4.3) | 542 | (4.1) | 559 | (4.2) | 559 | (6.1) |
| Manitoba | S | S | 455 | (9.4) | 503 | (5.7) | 517 | (4.7) | 540 | (4.4) | 563 | (5.5) | 571 | (5.9) |
| Saskatchewan | S | S | 472 | (8.5) | 500 | (5.5) | 519 | (3.7) | 544 | (4.4) | 557 | (5.0) | 548 | (5.8) |
| Alberta | S | S | 472 | (8.5) | 520 | (6.1) | 537 | (4.9) | 561 | (4.3) | 579 | (4.6) | 581 | (6.0) |
| British Columbia | S | S | 473 | (9.4) | 506 | (4.6) | 528 | (4.3) | 547 | (4.2) | 565 | (4.7) | 566 | (6.0) |
| **B. MATHEMATICS** | | | | | | | | | | | | | | |
| **CANADA** | **459** | **(9.9)** | **492** | **(4.4)** | **512** | **(2.8)** | **527** | **(2.2)** | **543** | **(2.0)** | **552** | **(2.2)** | **556** | **(3.3)** |
| France | 430 | (11.6) | 467 | (6.3) | 500 | (3.9) | 523 | (4.1) | 541 | (3.9) | 560 | (4.3) | 544 | (8.2) |
| United States | 392 | (15.0) | 423 | (11.1) | 469 | (8.6) | 497 | (7.0) | 514 | (7.9) | 547 | (8.3) | 554 | (7.8) |
| United Kingdom | 436 | (19.7) | 460 | (6.4) | 506 | (3.7) | 524 | (3.9) | 545 | (4.4) | 566 | (4.2) | 579 | (5.3) |
| Germany | S | S | 381 | (12.0) | 454 | (4.8) | 477 | (4.9) | 507 | (4.2) | 541 | (4.5) | 550 | (5.6) |
| Japan | 486 | (25.6) | 531 | (7.7) | 540 | (6.7) | 555 | (5.7) | 576 | (5.4) | 579 | (5.2) | 593 | (9.8) |
| Italy | S | S | 405 | (8.6) | 439 | (4.8) | 455 | (4.4) | 474 | (4.6) | 479 | (5.7) | 496 | (8.6) |
| Russian Federation | 356 | (26.5) | 414 | (9.8) | 450 | (7.7) | 460 | (5.8) | 492 | (6.0) | 515 | (6.6) | 512 | (5.6) |
| Australia | 498 | (16.7) | 474 | (9.5) | 508 | (5.0) | 516 | (4.5) | 543 | (5.4) | 554 | (5.6) | 561 | (6.7) |
| Belgium | 425 | (12.2) | 463 | (7.0) | 514 | (5.5) | 523 | (5.3) | 552 | (4.5) | 568 | (5.0) | 571 | (6.8) |
| Finland | S | S | 508 | (6.8) | 527 | (3.2) | 527 | (3.1) | 549 | (3.8) | 559 | (4.4) | 565 | (7.2) |
| Mexico | 328 | (6.9) | 365 | (3.7) | 383 | (3.6) | 409 | (4.9) | 429 | (7.3) | 458 | (9.7) | 426 | (17.2) |
| Sweden | S | S | 442 | (9.4) | 474 | (5.2) | 497 | (4.9) | 513 | (4.5) | 541 | (4.2) | 543 | (5.2) |
| Switzerland | 468 | (16.8) | 456 | (7.0) | 497 | (5.8) | 518 | (5.3) | 553 | (5.3) | 570 | (5.9) | 581 | (8.4) |
| Newfoundland | S | S | 468 | (12.9) | 492 | (6.4) | 500 | (5.5) | 521 | (5.7) | 521 | (8.2) | 525 | (6.9) |
| Prince Edward Island | S | S | 469 | (11.1) | 500 | (6.2) | 499 | (6.3) | 524 | (6.1) | 535 | (7.7) | 527 | (6.8) |
| Nova Scotia | S | S | 468 | (15.7) | 484 | (7.2) | 498 | (5.7) | 516 | (4.5) | 534 | (5.2) | 539 | (8.2) |
| New Brunswick | S | S | 467 | (8.3) | 491 | (4.7) | 501 | (5.0) | 517 | (3.9) | 526 | (4.9) | 521 | (6.4) |
| Quebec | 473 | (13.6) | 513 | (7.3) | 538 | (4.4) | 554 | (4.8) | 564 | (3.9) | 577 | (5.1) | 577 | (5.9) |
| Ontario | S | S | 476 | (7.9) | 492 | (6.0) | 512 | (4.3) | 536 | (4.1) | 543 | (4.9) | 546 | (6.7) |
| Manitoba | S | S | 469 | (11.9) | 504 | (5.4) | 533 | (5.3) | 542 | (6.1) | 564 | (6.9) | 563 | (8.0) |
| Saskatchewan | S | S | 473 | (9.1) | 504 | (6.7) | 522 | (5.6) | 536 | (4.8) | 542 | (5.3) | 538 | (7.9) |
| Alberta | S | S | 495 | (12.7) | 516 | (6.5) | 534 | (5.4) | 560 | (5.3) | 564 | (5.1) | 575 | (5.9) |
| British Columbia | S | S | 475 | (11.2) | 511 | (5.5) | 527 | (5.3) | 536 | (4.5) | 556 | (4.7) | 561 | (6.4) |

## TABLE 3.6 (Continued)

### Average Achievement Scores in Reading, Mathematics and Science by Number of Books at Home

| Country and province | None | | 1–10 | | 11–50 | | 51–100 | | 101–250 | | 251–500 | | More than 500 | |
|---|---|---|---|---|---|---|---|---|---|---|---|---|---|---|
| | | | | | | | **C. SCIENCE** | | | | | | | |
| **CANADA** | 434 | (11.6) | 477 | (4.3) | 506 | (3.2) | 526 | (2.4) | 539 | (2.3) | 554 | (2.6) | 554 | (3.3) |
| France | 410 | (10.2) | 436 | (7.0) | 480 | (5.0) | 505 | (4.6) | 534 | (4.5) | 553 | (5.6) | 549 | (7.0) |
| United States | 388 | (14.0) | 427 | (8.3) | 473 | (7.4) | 505 | (6.7) | 530 | (6.5) | 550 | (8.9) | 556 | (11.4) |
| United Kingdom | 414 | (13.7) | 462 | (6.7) | 502 | (4.5) | 521 | (3.4) | 555 | (4.4) | 578 | (4.4) | 586 | (6.0) |
| Germany | 393 | (18.7) | 393 | (10.3) | 448 | (5.0) | 478 | (5.5) | 513 | (4.6) | 534 | (4.5) | 555 | (6.5) |
| Japan | 475 | (19.9) | 516 | (8.1) | 539 | (6.6) | 547 | (5.7) | 569 | (5.7) | 574 | (6.1) | 598 | (7.8) |
| Italy | S | S | 421 | (11.2) | 461 | (5.7) | 470 | (4.7) | 498 | (4.2) | 509 | (6.4) | 517 | (6.9) |
| Russian Federation | S | S | 407 | (6.8) | 429 | (6.4) | 443 | (7.7) | 477 | (4.8) | 488 | (6.3) | 499 | (6.0) |
| Australia | 455 | (23.3) | 457 | (12.9) | 488 | (5.1) | 516 | (5.3) | 533 | (5.8) | 556 | (5.1) | 559 | (6.8) |
| Belgium | 387 | (15.8) | 439 | (6.4) | 484 | (4.7) | 500 | (6.5) | 529 | (4.7) | 554 | (4.9) | 547 | (8.0) |
| Finland | S | S | 498 | (6.7) | 521 | (3.4) | 530 | (3.7) | 551 | (4.0) | 570 | (5.1) | 565 | (8.8) |
| Mexico | 372 | (7.0) | 396 | (3.4) | 424 | (3.9) | 435 | (4.3) | 451 | (7.7) | 495 | (11.3) | 460 | (13.3) |
| Sweden | S | S | 451 | (13.4) | 473 | (5.0) | 496 | (4.7) | 519 | (4.3) | 534 | (5.0) | 549 | (5.0) |
| Switzerland | 417 | (18.9) | 417 | (7.3) | 455 | (5.7) | 483 | (5.3) | 515 | (5.3) | 549 | (5.5) | 549 | (9.9) |
| Newfoundland | S | S | 442 | (15.1) | 492 | (6.8) | 510 | (7.2) | 525 | (6.3) | 538 | (7.9) | 541 | (8.5) |
| Prince Edward Island | S | S | 464 | (12.9) | 485 | (5.9) | 496 | (6.1) | 522 | (6.6) | 527 | (5.8) | 541 | (9.3) |
| Nova Scotia | S | S | 463 | (13.2) | 487 | (7.9) | 500 | (5.0) | 518 | (5.6) | 545 | (5.1) | 539 | (8.2) |
| New Brunswick | S | S | 446 | (9.0) | 479 | (4.7) | 492 | (4.5) | 504 | (4.5) | 519 | (5.6) | 529 | (7.1) |
| Quebec | 440 | (17.1) | 494 | (7.2) | 528 | (5.5) | 547 | (5.1) | 564 | (4.7) | 562 | (6.4) | 563 | (7.5) |
| Ontario | S | S | 462 | (9.4) | 489 | (6.7) | 518 | (5.0) | 529 | (4.5) | 548 | (5.3) | 546 | (6.7) |
| Manitoba | S | S | 460 | (9.1) | 502 | (6.5) | 515 | (5.6) | 535 | (5.5) | 562 | (5.5) | 561 | (7.9) |
| Saskatchewan | S | S | 470 | (9.7) | 499 | (7.0) | 507 | (4.3) | 536 | (5.7) | 546 | (6.9) | 543 | (8.1) |
| Alberta | S | S | 480 | (12.1) | 516 | (6.8) | 536 | (5.5) | 553 | (5.0) | 575 | (5.0) | 580 | (7.6) |
| British Columbia | S | S | 473 | (12.0) | 501 | (5.4) | 523 | (4.8) | 543 | (4.0) | 556 | (5.7) | 559 | (7.5) |

## TABLE 3.7

### Effects of Family Educational Support on Achievement Scores in Reading, Mathematics and Science

| Country and province | Standardized Effect | | | Country and province | Standardized Effect | | |
|---|---|---|---|---|---|---|---|
| | Reading | Mathematics | Science | | Reading | Mathematics | Science |
| **CANADA** | **-0.08** | **-0.12** | **-0.11** | Sweden | -0.11 | -0.12 | -0.13 |
| | | | | Switzerland | -0.06 | -0.08 | -0.07 |
| France | -0.21 | -0.21 | -0.19 | Newfoundland | -0.11 | -0.17 | -0.15 |
| United States | -0.13 | -0.13 | -0.12 | Prince Edward Island | -0.07 | -0.10 | -0.11 |
| United Kingdom | -0.13 | -0.14 | -0.16 | Nova Scotia | -0.08 | -0.11 | -0.10 |
| Germany | -0.15 | -0.18 | -0.14 | New Brunswick | -0.08 | -0.08 | -0.10 |
| Japan | 0.11 | 0.08 | 0.13 | Quebec | -0.13 | -0.14 | -0.18 |
| Italy | -0.14 | -0.18 | -0.15 | Ontario | -0.07 | -0.11 | -0.08 |
| Russian Federation | -0.17 | -0.13 | -0.13 | Manitoba | -0.06 | -0.10 | -0.11 |
| Australia | -0.02 | -0.03 | -0.05 | Saskatchewan | -0.08 | -0.16 | -0.13 |
| Belgium | -0.20 | -0.21 | -0.17 | Alberta | -0.04 | -0.08 | -0.06 |
| Finland | -0.07 | -0.09 | -0.15 | British Columbia | -0.09 | -0.12 | -0.11 |
| Mexico | -0.09 | -0.10 | -0.09 | | | | |

## TABLE 3.8

### Effects of Parental Academic Interest and Parental Social Interest on Achievement Scores in Reading, Mathematics and Science

| Country and province | Standardized Effect | | Country and province | Standardized Effect | |
|---|---|---|---|---|---|
| | Parental academic interest | Parental social interest | | Parental academic interest | Parental social interest |
| **A. READING** | | | **C. SCIENCE** | | |
| **CANADA** | **0.22** | **0.14** | **CANADA** | **0.20** | **0.10** |
| France | 0.23 | 0.13 | France | 0.23 | 0.12 |
| United States | 0.22 | 0.14 | United States | 0.22 | 0.12 |
| United Kingdom | 0.26 | 0.14 | United Kingdom | 0.23 | 0.11 |
| Germany | 0.23 | 0.07 | Germany | 0.20 | 0.05 |
| Japan | 0.24 | 0.25 | Japan | 0.23 | 0.21 |
| Italy | 0.19 | 0.07 | Italy | 0.15 | 0.04 |
| Russian Federation | 0.17 | 0.14 | Russian Federation | 0.14 | 0.09 |
| Australia | 0.31 | 0.17 | Australia | 0.24 | 0.10 |
| Belgium | 0.14 | 0.10 | Belgium | 0.14 | 0.07 |
| Finland | 0.25 | 0.07 | Finland | 0.18 | 0.02 |
| Mexico | 0.26 | 0.18 | Mexico | 0.25 | 0.16 |
| Sweden | 0.25 | 0.06 | Sweden | 0.20 | 0.01 |
| Switzerland | 0.27 | 0.13 | Switzerland | 0.27 | 0.10 |
| Newfoundland | 0.24 | 0.15 | Newfoundland | 0.20 | 0.08 |
| Prince Edward Island | 0.27 | 0.20 | Prince Edward Island | 0.26 | 0.18 |
| Nova Scotia | 0.25 | 0.15 | Nova Scotia | 0.22 | 0.15 |
| New Brunswick | 0.21 | 0.12 | New Brunswick | 0.20 | 0.06 |
| Quebec | 0.15 | 0.07 | Quebec | 0.13 | -0.01 |
| Ontario | 0.24 | 0.15 | Ontario | 0.23 | 0.12 |
| Manitoba | 0.23 | 0.16 | Manitoba | 0.15 | 0.12 |
| Saskatchewan | 0.23 | 0.17 | Saskatchewan | 0.21 | 0.14 |
| Alberta | 0.27 | 0.22 | Alberta | 0.25 | 0.21 |
| British Columbia | 0.24 | 0.14 | British Columbia | 0.21 | 0.07 |

| Country and province | Parental academic interest | Parental social interest |
|---|---|---|
| **B. MATHEMATICS** | | |
| **CANADA** | **0.18** | **0.07** |
| France | 0.15 | 0.10 |
| United States | 0.20 | 0.15 |
| United Kingdom | 0.21 | 0.09 |
| Germany | 0.16 | 0.00 |
| Japan | 0.19 | 0.17 |
| Italy | 0.09 | 0.03 |
| Russian Federation | 0.12 | 0.11 |
| Australia | 0.25 | 0.15 |
| Belgium | 0.10 | 0.06 |
| Finland | 0.17 | 0.05 |
| Mexico | 0.21 | 0.13 |
| Sweden | 0.18 | -0.04 |
| Switzerland | 0.19 | 0.06 |
| Newfoundland | 0.16 | 0.03 |
| Prince Edward Island | 0.19 | 0.11 |
| Nova Scotia | 0.18 | 0.08 |
| New Brunswick | 0.14 | 0.06 |
| Quebec | 0.12 | 0.02 |
| Ontario | 0.19 | 0.05 |
| Manitoba | 0.21 | 0.12 |
| Saskatchewan | 0.16 | 0.08 |
| Alberta | 0.23 | 0.16 |
| British Columbia | 0.20 | 0.09 |

# TABLE 3.9

## Average Achievement Scores (in Reading, Mathematics and Science) of Students by Their Parents' Education Expectations

| Province | High school | Standard error | Trade school | Standard error | College | Standard error | One university | Standard error | More than one university | Standard error |
|---|---|---|---|---|---|---|---|---|---|---|
| | | | | **A. READING** | | | | | | |
| Newfoundland | 409 | (14.8) | 446 | (7.6) | 475 | (7.1) | 533 | (3.3) | 567 | (5.7) |
| Prince Edward Island | 443 | (13.4) | 450 | (10.0) | 481 | (7.0) | 535 | (3.3) | 557 | (6.6) |
| Nova Scotia | 435 | (12.4) | 448 | (6.8) | 494 | (4.9) | 537 | (2.7) | 564 | (5.8) |
| New Brunswick | 408 | (9.5) | 451 | (7.3) | 459 | (4.8) | 521 | (2.8) | 559 | (5.3) |
| Quebec | 451 | (8.4) | 485 | (6.1) | 523 | (4.3) | 558 | (3.0) | 570 | (5.4) |
| Ontario | 434 | (20.6) | 445 | (12.7) | 484 | (4.5) | 556 | (3.2) | 571 | (5.6) |
| Manitoba | 472 | (8.2) | 483 | (7.9) | 508 | (5.7) | 555 | (4.3) | 563 | (7.7) |
| Saskatchewan | 458 | (10.5) | 481 | (4.9) | 512 | (6.9) | 551 | (3.8) | 566 | (6.9) |
| Alberta | 448 | (13.7) | 489 | (7.9) | 522 | (4.8) | 574 | (3.4) | 599 | (5.6) |
| British Columbia | 454 | (15.3) | 472 | (6.3) | 505 | (4.9) | 557 | (3.1) | 576 | (5.4) |
| | | | | **B. MATHEMATICS** | | | | | | |
| Newfoundland | S | (15.6) | 461 | (8.4) | 475 | (6.8) | 523 | (4.3) | 545 | (6.5) |
| Prince Edward Island | S | (18.5) | 467 | (10.7) | 475 | (7.5) | 526 | (5.5) | 545 | (8.0) |
| Nova Scotia | 438 | (12.0) | 460 | (9.5) | 485 | (7.5) | 525 | (3.8) | 546 | (6.4) |
| New Brunswick | 441 | (12.1) | 473 | (8.0) | 479 | (5.5) | 521 | (3.0) | 545 | (6.0) |
| Quebec | 470 | (12.2) | 514 | (7.7) | 535 | (4.7) | 569 | (2.8) | 580 | (5.4) |
| Ontario | 449 | (23.6) | 462 | (13.6) | 482 | (4.6) | 541 | (3.4) | 553 | (6.0) |
| Manitoba | 495 | (11.3) | 505 | (9.9) | 509 | (7.0) | 555 | (4.4) | 559 | (8.2) |
| Saskatchewan | 479 | (10.9) | 495 | (5.5) | 520 | (8.5) | 540 | (3.7) | 562 | (8.9) |
| Alberta | 473 | (21.2) | 501 | (8.7) | 521 | (5.1) | 567 | (4.3) | 587 | (7.1) |
| British Columbia | S | (21.8) | 485 | (7.7) | 500 | (5.7) | 551 | (3.9) | 569 | (5.7) |
| | | | | **C. SCIENCE** | | | | | | |
| Newfoundland | S | (19.5) | 469 | (8.8) | 481 | (7.8) | 528 | (4.8) | 563 | (7.4) |
| Prince Edward Island | 446 | (14.3) | 470 | (12.9) | 484 | (8.4) | 518 | (3.9) | 547 | (8.1) |
| Nova Scotia | 439 | (15.9) | 454 | (9.0) | 493 | (5.8) | 533 | (4.3) | 551 | (7.5) |
| New Brunswick | 426 | (11.8) | 457 | (9.5) | 458 | (5.6) | 514 | (3.7) | 552 | (7.4) |
| Quebec | 465 | (8.7) | 498 | (6.8) | 530 | (5.0) | 562 | (4.0) | 570 | (6.8) |
| Ontario | 429 | (24.4) | 459 | (17.4) | 485 | (4.7) | 541 | (3.8) | 553 | (6.1) |
| Manitoba | 483 | (10.8) | 485 | (9.2) | 516 | (7.2) | 548 | (4.8) | 547 | (8.7) |
| Saskatchewan | 453 | (10.9) | 493 | (5.3) | 495 | (9.2) | 541 | (4.1) | 551 | (9.0) |
| Alberta | 467 | (16.2) | 505 | (8.8) | 516 | (5.8) | 566 | (3.8) | 590 | (6.9) |
| British Columbia | S | (21.7) | 490 | (8.3) | 504 | (6.4) | 546 | (3.6) | 566 | (5.9) |

## TABLE 3.10

### The Relative Impact of Family Factors on Achievement Scores in Reading, Mathematics and Science

| Family factors | CANADA | France | United States | United Kingdom | Germany | Japan | Italy | Russian Federation | Australia | Belgium | Finland | Mexico | Sweden | Switzerland | Newfoundland | Prince Edward Island | Nova Scotia | New Brunswick | Quebec | Ontario | Manitoba | Saskatchewan | Alberta | British Columbia |
|---|---|---|---|---|---|---|---|---|---|---|---|---|---|---|---|---|---|---|---|---|---|---|---|---|
| **A. READING** | | | | | | | | | | | | | | | | | | | | | | | | |
| Family structure | | | | S | | | | | | | | | | | | | | | | | | | | |
| Number of siblings | | | -s | -s | | | -s | | | -s | | | -s | | | | | | | | | | | |
| Socio-economic status | S | S | S | S | S | | S | S | S | S | S | S | S | S | S | S | S | S | S | S | S | | S | S |
| Family possessions | | | | | | | | | | | | | | | | | | | | | | | | |
| Number of books at home | S | S | S | S | S | S | S | S | | S | S | S | S | S | S | S | S | S | S | S | S | S | S | S |
| Home educational resources | | S | | S | | S | S | S | S | | S | | | | | | | | | | | | | |
| Home cultural possessions | | S | | | | S | | | S | | | | | | | | S | | | | | | | |
| Student's cultural activities | S | S | | S | S | S | | | | S | | | | | S | S | S | S | S | S | S | S | S | S |
| Family educational support | -s | -s | -s | -s | -s | | -s | -s | -s | -s | -s | -s | -s | -s | -s | -s | -s | -s | -s | -s | -s | -s | -s | -s |
| Parental academic interest | S | | | S | S | | S | | S | | S | S | S | | S | S | S | | | | S | S | S | S |
| Parental social interest | | | | | | S | | | | | | | | | | | S | | | | | | S | S |
| Language spoken at home | | | | | -s | | | | | | | -s | -s | | | | | -s | | -s | | | | -s |
| **B. MATHEMATICS** | | | | | | | | | | | | | | | | | | | | | | | | |
| Family structure | | | S | S | | | | | | | | | | | | | | | | | | | | |
| Number of siblings | | | -s | -s | | | -s | | | -s | | | -s | | | | | | | | | | | |
| Socio-economic status | S | S | S | S | S | | S | S | S | S | S | S | S | S | S | S | S | S | S | S | S | | S | S |
| Family possessions | | S | | | | | | | | | | | | | | | S | | | | | S | | |
| Number of books at home | S | S | S | S | S | S | S | S | | S | | S | S | S | S | S | S | S | S | S | S | S | S | S |
| Home educational resources | | S | | S | S | | S | | | | | S | S | S | | | S | | | | | | | |
| Home cultural possessions | | | | | | | | | | | | | | | | | | | | | | | | |
| Student's cultural activities | | | | S | S | | | | | S | | | | | S | S | | | S | S | | | | |
| Family educational support | -s | -s | -s | -s | -s | | -s | -s | -s | -s | -s | -s | -s | -s | -s | -s | -s | -s | -s | -s | -s | -s | -s | -s |
| Parental academic interest | S | | | | | | | S | | S | | S | S | | | | S | | | | S | S | S | S |
| Parental social interest | | | | | | | | | | | | | | | | | | | | | | | | |
| Language spoken at home | | | | | -s | | | | | | | -s | -s | | | | | | | | | | | |
| **C. SCIENCE** | | | | | | | | | | | | | | | | | | | | | | | | |
| Family structure | | | | | | | | | | | | | | S | | | | | | | | | | |
| Number of siblings | | -s | -s | -s | | | -s | | | -s | | | | | | | | | | | | -s | | |
| Socio-economic status | S | S | S | S | S | | S | S | S | S | S | S | S | S | S | S | S | S | S | S | S | | S | S |
| Family possessions | | | | | | | | | | | | | | | | | | | | | | | | |
| Number of books at home | S | S | S | S | S | S | S | S | S | S | S | S | S | S | S | S | S | S | S | S | S | S | S | S |
| Home educational resources | | S | | S | | | | | | S | S | S | | | | | | | | | | | | |
| Home cultural possessions | | | | | | | | | | S | | | | | | | S | | | | | | | |
| Student's cultural activities | S | | | S | S | | | | | S | | | | | S | S | | | S | S | | | S | S |
| Family educational support | -s | -s | -s | -s | -s | | -s | -s | -s | -s | -s | -s | -s | -s | -s | -s | -s | -s | -s | -s | -s | -s | -s | -s |
| Parental academic interest | S | | | S | | | | | | S | | S | | | | | S | S | S | S | | S | S | S |
| Parental social interest | | | | | | S | | | | | | | | | | | S | | | | | | | |
| Language spoken at home | -s | | | -s | | | | | | | -s | | -s | -s | | | | -s | | | | | | -s |

Note: In each domain, a multiple regression analysis was performed for each country and province. Significant effects are identified as small (s), moderate (m) or large (l), using the criteria outlined in the chapter. Variables with a negative effect are indicated with a "-" sign. Variables with trivial effect sizes, less than |0.10|, are not shown.

## TABLE 4.1

### Public School Enrolment, School Average Socio-economic Status and Family Possessions Effects on Individual Reading Achievement

| Country and province | Public School | | | School Average Socio-economic Status | | | School Average Family Possessions | | |
|---|---|---|---|---|---|---|---|---|---|
| | % of enrolment | Standard error | Standardized effect size | Average | Standard error | Standardized effect size | Average | Standard error | Standardized effect size |
| **CANADA** | **93.8** | **(0.7)** | **-0.46** | **52.8** | **(0.2)** | **0.27** | **0.41** | **(0.0)** | **0.23** |
| France | 77.8 | (3.3) | 0.01 | 48.0 | (0.6) | 0.48 | -0.15 | (0.0) | 0.41 |
| United States | 94.6 | (2.1) | -0.47 | 52.0 | (0.6) | 0.43 | 0.61 | (0.0) | 0.42 |
| United Kingdom | 90.8 | (1.6) | -0.93 | 51.0 | (0.4) | 0.42 | 0.42 | (0.0) | 0.27 |
| Germany | 95.9 | (1.4) | -0.69 | 48.7 | (0.5) | 0.62 | 0.20 | (0.0) | 0.40 |
| Japan | 69.6 | (4.0) | 0.10 | 50.3 | (0.6) | 0.21 | -0.14 | (0.0) | 0.18 |
| Italy | 94.1 | (1.9) | -0.27 | 47.0 | (0.6) | 0.49 | 0.12 | (0.0) | 0.30 |
| Russian Federation | 100.0 | (0.0) | N/A | 49.3 | (0.4) | 0.39 | -1.79 | (0.0) | 0.24 |
| Australia | .. | .. | .. | 52.1 | (0.5) | 0.36 | 0.42 | (0.0) | 0.27 |
| Belgium | 25.0 | (3.0) | -0.65 | 48.6 | (0.6) | 0.58 | -0.09 | (0.0) | 0.28 |
| Finland | 97.2 | (1.3) | -0.20 | 50.0 | (0.5) | 0.15 | 0.22 | (0.0) | 0.14 |
| Mexico | 85.1 | (2.8) | -0.82 | 42.1 | (0.7) | 0.56 | -1.44 | (0.1) | 0.51 |
| Sweden | 96.6 | (1.5) | 0.01 | 50.5 | (0.5) | 0.22 | 0.66 | (0.0) | 0.11 |
| Switzerland | 94.1 | (1.4) | -0.15 | 49.1 | (0.5) | 0.44 | 0.05 | (0.0) | 0.13 |
| Newfoundland | 100.0 | (0.0) | N/A | 47.5 | (1.5) | 0.25 | -0.06 | (0.1) | 0.19 |
| Prince Edward Island | 100.0 | (0.0) | N/A | 49.6 | (2.4) | 0.28 | 0.13 | (0.1) | 0.23 |
| Nova Scotia | 99.8 | (0.8) | S | 51.6 | (1.0) | 0.23 | 0.19 | (0.0) | 0.18 |
| New Brunswick | 100.0 | (0.0) | N/A | 50.0 | (1.1) | 0.21 | 0.11 | (0.0) | 0.20 |
| Quebec | 84.3 | (2.3) | -0.51 | 51.5 | (0.4) | 0.27 | 0.06 | (0.0) | 0.19 |
| Ontario | 97.9 | (0.7) | -0.71 | 54.1 | (0.3) | 0.30 | 0.56 | (0.0) | 0.26 |
| Manitoba | 93.2 | (4.1) | -0.65 | 50.3 | (1.0) | 0.25 | 0.32 | (0.1) | 0.32 |
| Saskatchewan | 97.1 | (2.6) | -0.48 | 51.0 | (0.9) | 0.12 | 0.52 | (0.0) | 0.20 |
| Alberta | 97.8 | (1.4) | 0.41 | 54.0 | (0.6) | 0.28 | 0.72 | (0.0) | 0.27 |
| British Columbia | 91.1 | (2.4) | -0.27 | 53.3 | (0.5) | 0.25 | 0.56 | (0.0) | 0.14 |

## TABLE 4.2

### Average Scores of School Climate Indicators and
### Effects on Individual Reading Achievement

| Country and province | Disciplinary Climate | | | Student Behaviour | | |
|---|---|---|---|---|---|---|
| | Average | Standard error | Standardized effect size | Average | Standard error | Standardized effect size |
| **CANADA** | **0.14** | **(0.0)** | **-0.11** | **0.27** | **(0.0)** | **-0.10** |
| France | 0.05 | (0.0) | -0.03 | -0.18 | (0.1) | -0.14 |
| United States | -0.02 | (0.0) | -0.12 | 0.23 | (0.1) | -0.10 |
| United Kingdom | -0.02 | (0.0) | -0.20 | -0.04 | (0.1) | -0.33 |
| Germany | -0.10 | (0.0) | -0.15 | 0.10 | (0.1) | -0.29 |
| Japan | -0.49 | (0.0) | -0.37 | -0.69 | (0.1) | -0.39 |
| Italy | 0.24 | (0.0) | -0.29 | -0.18 | (0.1) | -0.37 |
| Russian Federation | -0.44 | (0.0) | -0.16 | 0.96 | (0.1) | -0.11 |
| Australia | 0.09 | (0.0) | -0.21 | -0.06 | (0.1) | -0.23 |
| Belgium | 0.11 | (0.0) | -0.03 | -0.26 | (0.1) | -0.45 |
| Finland | 0.16 | (0.0) | -0.05 | 0.42 | (0.0) | -0.03 |
| Mexico | -0.17 | (0.0) | 0.04 | 0.05 | (0.1) | -0.04 |
| Sweden | 0.19 | (0.0) | -0.15 | 0.05 | (0.1) | -0.12 |
| Switzerland | -0.30 | (0.0) | -0.12 | 0.01 | (0.1) | -0.10 |
| Newfoundland | 0.14 | (0.1) | -0.06 | 0.33 | (0.2) | -0.05 |
| Prince Edward Island | 0.16 | (0.1) | -0.15 | 0.70 | (0.4) | 0.01 |
| Nova Scotia | 0.21 | (0.1) | -0.13 | 0.38 | (0.1) | -0.04 |
| New Brunswick | 0.19 | (0.1) | -0.05 | 0.68 | (0.1) | 0.17 |
| Quebec | 0.08 | (0.0) | -0.09 | 0.19 | (0.1) | -0.07 |
| Ontario | 0.16 | (0.0) | -0.09 | 0.30 | (0.0) | -0.12 |
| Manitoba | 0.23 | (0.1) | -0.13 | 0.23 | (0.1) | -0.17 |
| Saskatchewan | 0.13 | (0.1) | -0.11 | 0.25 | (0.1) | -0.14 |
| Alberta | 0.15 | (0.0) | -0.17 | 0.28 | (0.1) | -0.13 |
| British Columbia | 0.11 | (0.0) | -0.13 | 0.19 | (0.1) | -0.09 |

## TABLE 4.3

### Average Scores of Teacher-student Interaction Indicators and Effects on Individual Reading Achievement

| Country and province | Negative Teacher Behaviour | | | Teacher Support | | | Teacher-student Relations | | |
|---|---|---|---|---|---|---|---|---|---|
| | Average | Standard error | Standardized effect size | Average | Standard error | Standardized effect size | Average | Standard error | Standardized effect size |
| **CANADA** | **-0.12** | **(0.0)** | **-0.04** | **0.31** | **(0.0)** | **-0.01** | **0.25** | **(0.0)** | **0.05** |
| France | 0.00 | (0.1) | -0.07 | -0.20 | (0.0) | -0.10 | -0.05 | (0.0) | -0.02 |
| United States | 0.07 | (0.1) | -0.09 | 0.35 | (0.0) | -0.01 | 0.20 | (0.0) | 0.19 |
| United Kingdom | 0.08 | (0.1) | -0.20 | 0.50 | (0.0) | 0.07 | 0.25 | (0.0) | 0.12 |
| Germany | 0.16 | (0.1) | -0.07 | -0.34 | (0.0) | -0.33 | -0.21 | (0.0) | -0.05 |
| Japan | -0.12 | (0.1) | -0.20 | -0.17 | (0.0) | 0.09 | -0.32 | (0.0) | 0.33 |
| Italy | -0.05 | (0.1) | -0.09 | -0.28 | (0.0) | -0.20 | -0.15 | (0.0) | -0.07 |
| Russian Federation | 0.75 | (0.1) | -0.06 | 0.16 | (0.0) | 0.04 | 0.04 | (0.0) | -0.02 |
| Australia | 0.11 | (0.1) | -0.16 | 0.42 | (0.0) | 0.05 | 0.17 | (0.0) | 0.15 |
| Belgium | -0.07 | (0.1) | -0.25 | -0.28 | (0.0) | -0.18 | 0.01 | (0.0) | -0.05 |
| Finland | 0.08 | (0.1) | 0.04 | 0.02 | (0.0) | 0.00 | -0.08 | (0.0) | -0.02 |
| Mexico | 0.65 | (0.1) | 0.02 | 0.07 | (0.0) | -0.10 | 0.55 | (0.0) | -0.01 |
| Sweden | 0.00 | (0.1) | -0.03 | 0.21 | (0.0) | 0.02 | 0.12 | (0.0) | 0.04 |
| Switzerland | -0.13 | (0.0) | 0.06 | 0.01 | (0.0) | -0.22 | 0.25 | (0.0) | 0.00 |
| Newfoundland | -0.22 | (0.2) | -0.03 | 0.43 | (0.1) | 0.02 | 0.46 | (0.1) | 0.11 |
| Prince Edward Island | 0.14 | (0.4) | 0.03 | 0.35 | (0.1) | -0.05 | 0.30 | (0.1) | 0.08 |
| Nova Scotia | -0.10 | (0.1) | -0.02 | 0.38 | (0.0) | 0.04 | 0.39 | (0.1) | 0.07 |
| New Brunswick | 0.24 | (0.1) | -0.04 | 0.21 | (0.1) | -0.02 | 0.18 | (0.1) | -0.01 |
| Quebec | 0.27 | (0.1) | -0.02 | 0.33 | (0.0) | -0.03 | 0.28 | (0.0) | 0.06 |
| Ontario | -0.37 | (0.0) | -0.09 | 0.31 | (0.0) | -0.01 | 0.23 | (0.0) | 0.02 |
| Manitoba | 0.02 | (0.1) | -0.08 | 0.36 | (0.0) | -0.03 | 0.26 | (0.1) | 0.04 |
| Saskatchewan | -0.18 | (0.1) | -0.02 | 0.40 | (0.1) | 0.04 | 0.28 | (0.0) | 0.13 |
| Alberta | -0.15 | (0.1) | -0.01 | 0.25 | (0.0) | -0.04 | 0.27 | (0.0) | 0.08 |
| British Columbia | -0.16 | (0.1) | -0.03 | 0.23 | (0.0) | 0.02 | 0.17 | (0.0) | 0.06 |

## TABLE 4.4

### Average Scores of School Resource Indicators and Effects on Individual Reading Achievement

| Country and province | Teacher Shortage | | | Teacher Morale and Commitment | | | Inadequacy of Instructional Resources | | | Inadequacy of Material Resources | | |
|---|---|---|---|---|---|---|---|---|---|---|---|---|
| | Average | Stan-dard error | Stan-dardized effect size | Average | Stan-dard error | Stan-dardized effect size | Average | Stan-dard error | Stan-dardized effect size | Average | Stan-dard error | Stan-dardized effect size |
| **CANADA** | **0.01** | **(0.0)** | **-0.04** | **0.08** | **(0.0)** | **0.04** | **-0.24** | **(0.0)** | **-0.06** | **-0.35** | **(0.0)** | **-0.01** |
| France | -0.33 | (0.1) | -0.04 | 0.06 | (0.1) | 0.14 | -0.48 | (0.1) | -0.10 | -0.63 | (0.1) | 0.03 |
| United States | -0.20 | (0.1) | -0.10 | -0.04 | (0.1) | 0.10 | -0.40 | (0.1) | -0.01 | -0.20 | (0.1) | 0.02 |
| United Kingdom | 0.40 | (0.1) | -0.18 | 0.02 | (0.1) | 0.15 | 0.44 | (0.1) | -0.11 | 0.41 | (0.1) | -0.06 |
| Germany | 0.23 | (0.1) | -0.27 | -0.01 | (0.1) | 0.06 | 0.20 | (0.1) | -0.14 | -0.14 | (0.1) | -0.06 |
| Japan | 0.23 | (0.1) | -0.14 | 0.14 | (0.1) | 0.27 | 0.00 | (0.1) | -0.13 | 0.21 | (0.1) | -0.04 |
| Italy | 0.28 | (0.1) | 0.02 | -0.69 | (0.1) | 0.05 | -0.07 | (0.1) | -0.14 | 0.20 | (0.1) | -0.05 |
| Russian Federation | 0.75 | (0.1) | -0.03 | -0.15 | (0.1) | 0.17 | 1.27 | (0.1) | -0.13 | 0.52 | (0.1) | -0.13 |
| Australia | 0.18 | (0.1) | -0.17 | 0.04 | (0.1) | 0.16 | -0.28 | (0.1) | -0.10 | -0.05 | (0.1) | -0.03 |
| Belgium | -0.25 | (0.1) | -0.13 | -0.20 | (0.1) | 0.27 | -0.45 | (0.1) | -0.08 | -0.33 | (0.1) | -0.13 |
| Finland | -0.09 | (0.1) | -0.01 | 0.02 | (0.1) | 0.06 | 0.22 | (0.1) | 0.04 | 0.22 | (0.1) | 0.03 |
| Mexico | 0.53 | (0.1) | -0.05 | 0.39 | (0.1) | 0.06 | 0.95 | (0.1) | -0.35 | 0.39 | (0.1) | -0.22 |
| Sweden | 0.25 | (0.1) | -0.08 | 0.34 | (0.1) | 0.06 | 0.00 | (0.1) | -0.07 | -0.01 | (0.1) | -0.06 |
| Switzerland | -0.35 | (0.0) | -0.09 | 0.43 | (0.1) | 0.02 | -0.51 | (0.1) | -0.08 | -0.49 | (0.0) | 0.00 |
| Newfoundland | 0.60 | (0.2) | 0.05 | 0.03 | (0.2) | -0.02 | 0.39 | (0.2) | 0.01 | -0.16 | (0.2) | 0.03 |
| Prince Edward Island | 0.99 | (0.5) | 0.05 | 0.76 | (0.3) | -0.09 | 0.08 | (0.4) | -0.05 | -0.35 | (0.3) | -0.02 |
| Nova Scotia | 0.75 | (0.2) | 0.00 | -0.06 | (0.2) | 0.07 | 0.54 | (0.1) | 0.06 | 0.20 | (0.2) | 0.06 |
| New Brunswick | 0.58 | (0.2) | 0.08 | -0.07 | (0.2) | 0.04 | 0.03 | (0.2) | -0.03 | -0.25 | (0.2) | -0.07 |
| Quebec | -0.12 | (0.1) | -0.01 | -0.05 | (0.1) | 0.05 | -0.65 | (0.1) | -0.08 | -0.61 | (0.0) | -0.06 |
| Ontario | -0.09 | (0.1) | -0.03 | -0.01 | (0.0) | 0.10 | -0.16 | (0.1) | -0.08 | -0.38 | (0.0) | 0.00 |
| Manitoba | 0.27 | (0.2) | -0.13 | 0.14 | (0.1) | 0.00 | 0.13 | (0.1) | -0.07 | -0.19 | (0.1) | 0.03 |
| Saskatchewan | 0.26 | (0.1) | 0.00 | 0.47 | (0.2) | 0.02 | -0.16 | (0.1) | 0.00 | -0.30 | (0.1) | 0.00 |
| Alberta | 0.34 | (0.1) | 0.01 | 0.39 | (0.1) | 0.02 | -0.16 | (0.1) | -0.03 | 0.00 | (0.1) | 0.03 |
| British Columbia | -0.28 | (0.1) | -0.04 | 0.24 | (0.1) | -0.02 | -0.25 | (0.1) | -0.01 | -0.34 | (0.1) | -0.02 |

## TABLE 4.5

### The Relative Impact of School Factors on Reading Achievement Scores

| | Country and province | | | | | | | | | | | | | | | | | | | | | | | |
|---|---|---|---|---|---|---|---|---|---|---|---|---|---|---|---|---|---|---|---|---|---|---|---|---|
| | CANADA | France | United States | United Kingdom | Germany | Japan | Italy | Russian Federation | Australia | Belgium | Finland | Mexico | Sweden | Switzerland | Newfoundland | Prince Edward Island | Nova Scotia | New Brunswick | Quebec | Ontario | Manitoba | Saskatchewan | Alberta | British Columbia |
| Public school | | | | | | | | | | -m | | m | | m | | | * | | | s | | | m | |
| School average socio-economic status | s | m | s | m | m | s | s | m | s | l | | m | s | m | s | s | s | | s | s | | | s | s |
| School average family possessions | s | s | s | | s | | | | | -s | | s | | | | | | s | s | s | s | | | |
| Disciplinary climate | | | | | | -s | -s | -s | -s | | | -s | | | | | -s | | | -s | | | -s | |
| Student behaviour | | | -s | | -m | -s | | | | -s | | | | -s | | | | | s | | | | | |
| Negative teacher behaviour | | | | | | s | | | | | | | | s | | | | | | | | | | |
| Teacher support | | -s | | -s | | -s | | | | -s | | | | -s | | | | | | | | | | |
| Teacher-student relations | | | | | | s | | | | | | | | | | | | s | | | | | | |
| Teacher shortage | | | | | | -s | s | | | | | | | | | | | | | | | | | |
| Teacher morale and commitment | | | | | | s | | | | | | | | | | | | | | | | | | |
| Inadequacy of instructional resources | | -s | | | | | -s | | | | | | | | | | | | | | | | | |
| Inadequacy of material resources | s | | | | | | | | | | | | | | | | | | | | | | | |

Note: In each domain, a multiple regression analysis was performed for each country and province. For each variable, significant effects are identified as small (s), moderate (m) or large (l), using the criteria outlined in the chapter. Variables with a negative effect are indicated with a "-" sign. Variables with trivial effect sizes, less than 0.10, are not shown. Effects of school variables on student achievement in Finland were all trivial or insignificant.

* Estimates suppressed due to small sample sizes.

# Annex B

# Definitions of Key Variables and Constructs

For detailed information on the technical and methodological background of PISA, see Annex A of the international OECD report *Knowledge and Skills for Life – First results from the OECD Programme for International Student Assessment.*

**Note:** Several of the measures in this report reflect indices that summarise responses from students or school representatives (typically principals) to a series of related questions. It is important to note that negative values in an index do not necessarily imply that students responded negatively to the underlying questions. A negative value merely indicates that a group of students (or all students, collectively, in a single country) or principals responded less positively than all students or principals did on average across OECD countries. Likewise, a positive value on an index indicates that a group of students or principals responded more favourably, or more positively, than students or principals did, on average, in OECD countries.

## Chapter 1:

**Reading literacy** is defined in PISA as the ability to understand, use and reflect on written texts in order to achieve one's goals, to develop one's knowledge and potential, and to participate effectively in society. This definition goes beyond the notion that reading literacy means decoding written material and literal comprehension. Reading incorporates understanding and reflecting on texts. Literacy involves the ability of individuals to use written information to fulfil their goals, and the consequent ability of complex modern societies to use written information to function effectively.

The concept of reading literacy in PISA has three dimensions, which have guided the development of the assessment: the type of reading task, the form and structure of the reading material, and the use for which the text was constructed. Personal competence is best understood in terms of the first of these. The other two are properties of the task materials that were helpful in ensuring that a range of diverse tasks were included in the tests.

The 'type of reading task' dimension is measured on three scales. A "retrieving information" scale reports on students' ability to locate information in a text. An "interpreting" scale reports on the ability to construct meaning and draw inferences from written information. A "reflection and evaluation" scale reports on students' ability to relate text to their knowledge, ideas and experiences. In addition, a combined reading literacy scale summarises the results from the three reading literacy scales.

**Mathematical literacy** is defined in PISA as the capacity to identify, understand and engage in mathematics, and to make well-founded judgements about the role that mathematics plays in an individual's current and future private life, occupational life, social life with peers and relatives, and life as a constructive, concerned and reflective citizen. As with reading, the definition revolves around the wider uses of mathematics in people's lives rather than being limited to mechanical operations. "Mathematical literacy" is used here to indicate the ability to put mathematical knowledge and skills to functional use rather than just mastering them within a school curriculum. To "engage in" mathematics covers not simply physical or social actions (such as deciding how much change to give someone in a shop) but also wider uses, including taking a point of view and appreciating things expressed mathematically (such as having an opinion about a government's spending plans). Mathematical literacy also implies the ability to pose and solve mathematical problems in a variety of situations, as well as the inclination to do so, which often relies on personal traits such as self-confidence and curiosity.

**Scientific literacy** relates to the ability to think scientifically in a world in which science and technology shape lives. Such literacy requires an understanding of scientific concepts as well as an ability to apply a scientific perspective. PISA defines scientific literacy as the capacity to use scientific knowledge, to identify questions, and to draw evidence-based conclusions in order to understand and help make decisions about the natural world and the changes made to it through human activity.

## Chapter 2:

**Reading enjoyment:** This index was derived from students' level of agreement with the following statements: I read only if I have to; reading is one of my favourite hobbies; I like talking about books with other people; I find it hard to finish books; I feel happy if I receive a book as a present; for me reading is a waste of time; I enjoy going to a bookstore or a library; I read only to get information that I need; and, I cannot sit still and read for more than a few minutes. The International OECD report refers to this variable as *engagement in reading*.

**Time spent reading for enjoyment:** This measures the amount of time a student spends *each day* reading for enjoyment. The categories range from not reading for enjoyment to more than two hours per day.

**Reading diversity:** This index is derived from students' reporting how often they read various types of materials for enjoyment: magazines, comic books, fiction, non-fiction, e-mail and webpages, and newspapers.

**Use of public and school libraries:** Students were asked how often they borrow books to read for pleasure from a public or school library.

**Homework time:** This index was derived from students' reports on the amount of time they devote to homework in the language of assessment, mathematics and science.

**Sense of belonging to school:** This index was derived from students' reports on their level of agreement with the following statements that school is a place where: I feel like an outsider, I make friends easily, I feel like I belong, I feel awkward and out of place, other students seem to like me, and I feel lonely.

**Student career expectations:** Students were asked to report what kind of job they expect to have when they are about thirty years old. This information was then classified by occupational status according to the *International Socio-Economic Index of Occupational Status (ISEI)* (defined under *socio-economic status*).

**Student education expectations:** This variable was collected as part of the Youth in Transition Survey (YITS). It is available only for Canada. Students reported what is the highest level of education they would like to get.

**School year job status:** This variable was collected as part of the Youth in Transition Survey (YITS). It is available only for Canada. Students were asked whether, since the beginning of the school year, they had done any work a) for pay from an employer, b) for pay at an odd job, or c) for a family farm or business (with or without pay).

**School year weekday and weekend work hours:** This variable was collected as part of the Youth in Transition Survey (YITS). It is available only for Canada. Students were asked how many hours in total they worked at all jobs and odd jobs, for a typical week, for weekdays, and weekends.

## Chapter 3:

**Family structure:** Students were asked to report who usually lived at home with them. The response categories were then grouped into four categories: *i) single parent family* (students who reported living with one of the following: mother, father, female guardian or male guardian); *ii) nuclear family* (students who reported living with a mother and a father); *iii) mixed family* (students who reported living with a mother and a male guardian, a father and a female guardian, or two guardians); and *iv) other response combinations.* For this analysis, two-parent families include both nuclear families and mixed families.

**Number of siblings:** Students were asked to indicate the number of siblings older than themselves, younger than themselves, or of the same age.

**Socio-economic status:** Students were asked to report their mother's and father's occupation, and to state whether each parent was: in full-time paid work; part-time paid work; not working but looking for a paid job; or "other". The open-ended responses were then coded in accordance with the International Standard Classification of Occupations (ISCO 1988).

The PISA *International Socio-Economic Index of Occupational Status (ISEI)* was derived from student responses on parental occupation. The index captures the attributes of occupations that convert parents' education into income. The index was derived by the optimal scaling of occupation groups to maximise the indirect effect of education on income through occupation and to minimise the direct effect of education on income, net of occupation (both effects being net of age). For more information on the methodology, see *Ganzeboom, de Graaf and Treiman (1992)*[1]. The PISA International Socio-Economic Index of Occupational Status is based on either the father's or mother's occupations, whichever is the higher.

In this report, socio-economic status is measured according to parental occupation. In the International OECD report, this analysis was carried out using a measure of socio-economic status, the *index of economic, social and cultural status*, which combines the ISEI with information on the highest level of education of the student's parents, family wealth, home educational resources, and family cultural possessions. In spite of the use of this different measure to look at socio-economic status, the results of the Canadian and International analysis are very similar.

**Family possessions:** This index was derived from students' reports on: *i)* the availability, in their home, of a dishwasher, a room of their own, educational software, and a link to the Internet; and *ii)* the number of cellular phones, television sets, computers, cars and bathrooms at home. In the International OECD report, this variable was referred to as *family wealth.*

**Number of books at home:** Students reported an estimate of how many books there are in their home. They were given a calculation that there are approximately 40 books per metre of shelving and were asked not to include magazines.

**Home educational resources:** This index was derived from students' reports on the availability and number of the following items in their home: a dictionary, a quiet place to study, a desk for study, textbooks and calculators.

**Home cultural possessions:** This index was derived from students' reports on the availability of the following items in their home: classical literature (examples were given), books of poetry and works of art (examples were given). The International OECD report refers to this variable as the *index of possessions related to "classical culture" in the family home.*

**Students' cultural activities:** This index was derived from students' reports on how often they had participated in the following activities during the preceding year: visited a museum or art gallery; attended an opera, ballet or classical symphony concert; and watched live theatre. In the International OECD report, this variable is referred to as the *index of activities related to "classical culture".*

**Family educational support:** This was derived from students' reports on how frequently the mother, the father, or brothers and sisters worked with the student on what is regarded nationally as school work.

**Parental academic interest:** The index of parental academic interest was derived from students' reports on the frequency with which their parents (or guardians) engaged with them in the following activities: discussing political or social issues; discussing books, films or television programmes; and listening to classical music. In the International OECD report, this variable is referred to as the *index of cultural communication.*

**Parental social interest:** This index was derived from students' reports on the frequency with which their parents (or guardians) engaged with them in the following activities: discussing how well they are doing at school; eating the evening meal with them around a table; and spending time simply talking with them. In the International OECD report, this variable is referred to as the *index of social communication.*

**Parent's education expectations:** This variable was collected as part of the Youth in Transition Survey (YITS). It is available only for Canada. Parents reported what is the highest level of education they hope their child will get.

**Language spoken at home:** Students were asked if the language spoken at home most of the time was the language of assessment, other official national language, other national dialects or languages or other languages. The responses were then grouped into two categories: *i)* the language spoken at home most of the time is different from the language of assessment, from other official national language and from other national dialects or languages, and *ii)* the language spoken at home most of the time is the language of assessment, other official national language or other national dialects or languages. For this analysis, the variable was further defined to identify students who were born outside the country and who spoke a language at home which was neither an official language nor a national dialect.

## Chapter 4:

**School type:** A school was classified as either public or private according to whether a public agency or a private entity had the ultimate power to make decisions concerning its affairs. A school was classified as *public* if the school principal reported that it was: controlled and managed directly by a public education authority or agency; or controlled and managed either by a government agency directly or by a governing body (council, committee, etc.), most of whose members were either appointed by a public authority or elected by public franchise. A school was classified as *private* if the school principal reported that it was controlled and managed by a non-governmental organisation (e.g., a church, a trade union or a business enterprise) or if its governing board consisted mostly of members not selected by a public agency. A distinction was made between "government-dependent" and "independent" private schools according to the degree of a private school's dependence on funding from government sources. School principals were asked to specify the percentage of the school's total funding received in a typical school year from: government sources; student fees or school charges paid by parents; donations, sponsorships or parental fund-raising; and other sources. Schools were classified as *government-dependent private* if they received 50 per cent or more of their core funding from

government agencies. Schools were classified as *independent private* if they received less than 50 per cent of their core funding from government agencies.

**School average socio-economic status:** This index measures the average of the highest socio-economic status (ISEI) of the parents reported by all students in a school. The variable was then used as a characteristic for each student as a measure of the average socio-economic status of their school.

**School average of family possessions:** This index measures the average of *family possessions index* derived for students in a school. The variable was then used as a characteristic for each student as a measure of the average family wealth (in terms of family possessions) of the population attending their school.

**Disciplinary climate:** This index summarises students' reports on the frequency with which, in their language class: the teacher has to wait a long time for students to quiet down; students cannot work well; students don't listen to what the teacher says; students don't start working for a long time after the lesson begins; there is noise and disorder; and, at the start of class, more than five minutes are spent doing nothing. In the International OECD report, this index was inverted so that low values indicate a poor disciplinary climate.

**Student behaviour:** This index summarises principals' perceptions of the school's disciplinary climate by reporting the extent to which learning by 15-year-olds in their school was hindered by: student absenteeism; disruption of classes by students; students skipping classes; students lacking respect for teachers; the use of alcohol or illegal drugs; and students intimidating or bullying other students. In the International OECD report, this variable was referred to as the *index of student-related factors affecting school climate* and was inverted so that low values indicate a poor disciplinary climate.

**Negative teacher behaviour:** This index was derived from principals' reports on the extent to which the learning by 15-year-olds was hindered by: the low expectations of teachers; poor student-teacher relations; teachers not meeting individual students' needs; teacher absenteeism; staff resisting change; teachers being too strict with students; and students not being encouraged to achieve their full potential. In the International OECD report, this variable was referred to as the *index of teacher-related factors affecting school climate* and was inverted so that low values indicate a poor disciplinary climate.

**Teacher support:** This index was derived from students' reports on the frequency with which: the teacher shows an interest in every student's learning; the teacher gives students an opportunity to express opinions; the teacher helps students with their work; the teacher continues teaching until the students understand; the teacher does a lot to help students; and, the teacher helps students with their learning.

**Teacher-student relations:** This index was derived from students' reports on their level of agreement with the following statements: students get along well with most teachers; most teachers are interested in students' well-being; most of my teachers really listen to what I have to say; if I need extra help, I will receive it from my teachers; and most of my teachers treat me fairly.

**Teacher shortage:** This index was derived from principals views on how much learning by 15-year-old students was hindered by the shortage or inadequacy of teachers in language classes, mathematics or science. In the International OECD report, this index was inverted so that low values indicate problems with teacher shortage.

**Teacher morale and commitment:** This index was derived from the extent to which school principals agreed with the following statements: the morale of the teachers in this school is high; teachers work with enthusiasm; teachers take pride in this school; and teachers value academic achievement.

**Inadequacy of instructional resources:** This index was derived based on the school principals' reports on the extent to which learning by 15-year-olds was hindered by: not enough computers for instruction; lack of instructional materials in the library; lack of multi-media resources for instruction; inadequate science laboratory equipment; and inadequate facilities for the fine arts. In the International OECD report, this variable was referred to as the *index of quality of a school's educational resources* and was inverted so that low values indicate a low quality of educational resources.

**Inadequacy of material resources:** This index was derived from principals' reports on the extent to which learning by 15-year-olds in their school was hindered by: poor condition of buildings; poor heating and cooling and/or lighting systems; and lack of instructional space (e.g., classrooms). In the International OECD report, this variable was referred to as the *index of the quality of a school's physical infrastructure* and was inverted so that low values indicate a low quality of physical infrastructure.

## Note

1. Ganzeboom, H.B.G., De Graaf, P., Treiman, D.J. (with De Leeuw, J.), (1992), "A Standard International Socio-Economic Index of Occupational Status", *Social Science Research*, 21(1), pp. 1-56.